D0887614

PRELUDE TO LEADERSHIP

The European Diary of John F. Kennedy

Summer 1945

PRELUDE TO LEADERSHIP

The European Diary of John F. Kennedy

Summer 1945

Introduction by Hugh Sidey

Regnery Publishing, Inc.
Washington, D.C.

Editor's Preface copyright © 1995 by Deirdre Henderson

Introduction copyright © 1995 by Hugh Sidey

All Rights Reserved
Manufactured in the United States of America

1995 Printing

No part of this book may be reproduced in any form by any electronic or mechanical means, including information storage and retrieval systems, without permission in writing from the publisher, except by a reviewer who may quote brief passages in review.

Library of Congress Cataloging-in-Publication Data

Kennedy, John F. (John Fitzgerald), 1917-1963.
    Prelude to Leadership : the European diary of John F. Kennedy,
summer 1945 / introduction by Hugh Sidey.
        p.   cm.
    Includes bibliographical references.
    ISBN 0-89526-459-5
    1. Kennedy, John F. (John Fitzgerald), 1917-1963—Diaries.
    2. Kennedy, John F. (John Fitzgerald), 1917-1963—Journeys—Europe.
    3. Europe—Description and travel. 4. Europe—History—1945-
    5. Presidents—United States—Diaries. I. Title.
    E842.1.A6S55   1995
    973.922 ' 092—dc20
    [B]   95-44279
                                                                                                CIP

Published in the United States of America by
Regnery Publishing, Inc.
An Eagle Publishing Company
422 First Street, S.E.
Washington, D.C. 20003

Distributed to the trade by
National Book Network
4720-A Boston Way
Lanham, MD 20706

10 9 8 7 6 5 4 3 2 1

Books are available in quantity for promotional or premium use. Write to Director of Special Sales, Regnery Publishing, Inc., 422 First Street, S.E., Washington, D.C. 20003, for information on discounts and terms or call (202) 546-5005.

DEDICATION

■

**THIS BOOK IS DEDICATED TO THOSE WHO
SERVED IN WORLD WAR II
AND TO THEIR SONS AND DAUGHTERS.**

When I think of how much this war has cost us,
of the deaths of Cy and Peter and Orv and Gil
and Demi and Joe and Billy and all those
thousands and millions who have died with them—
when I think of all those gallant acts that I have
seen or anyone who has been to war—it would be a
very easy thing for me to feel disappointed and
somewhat betrayed...

You have seen battlefields where sacrifice was
the order of the day and to compare that
sacrifice to the timidity and selfishness of the
nations gathered at San Francisco must
inevitably be disillusioning...*

Written by John F. Kennedy to a "PT-boat friend"
from the United Nations Conference in
San Francisco, June 1945.

* Partial text of letter in Arthur M. Schlesinger, Jr.'s book,
A Thousand Days.

TABLE OF CONTENTS

■

EDITOR'S PREFACE

■

In the summer of 1945 an energetic, thin and somewhat frail young man traveled to Europe—
England, Ireland, France, and Germany—as a
reporter for the Hearst newspapers. His assignment was
to cover the situation in Europe after the surrender of
Germany, following his attendance at the San Francisco
Conference, which established the United Nations. The
young man was a seasoned world traveler, a veteran of
World War II, and a well-educated professional who had
introductions to world leaders and friends in high
places.

The young man was John F. Kennedy, age 28, and
during the trip he kept a diary. In it he recorded his
impressions of the future of western democracies, the
economic conditions in Europe following the devastation of the war, as well as his predictions on the emerging cold war.

The diary gives us a short but precious look into the
mind of a man whose reasoning and insight were not

that of the average twenty-eight-year old. The diary, like so many of his early speeches, shows someone who is already a strong writer and an inquisitive and pragmatic thinker searching for solutions and quick to learn from others. He has an amazingly clear vision of how future world events would unfold. The diary certainly challenges the view that most of JFK's later writings were authored by others.

Many of the accounts of President Kennedy's life portray him as a late bloomer and a liberal, particularly on economic and social issues. Some of those who took over the job of defining Kennedy after his death reflected their own views, and portrayed him as one of their own. Moreover, the official legacy of the Kennedy years has been painted with nostalgia. Most biographers give the reader a taste of the Kennedy charisma, but too little has been told of the tough minded, intelligent student of history who believed he knew where the post-war world was headed and was intent on securing America's safety and leadership. The Kennedy years had their brief shining moments, but the bulk of JFK's presidency was taken up with the struggles and hard realities of the cold war. He witnessed the beginning of those post-war crises as a reporter in 1945 and recorded his thoughts in this diary, thoughts that reveal a Kennedy not entirely consistent with the image usually projected by his chroniclers.

Uncovered in these pages is clear evidence that, far from being a late bloomer, the speeches JFK gave in the 1950s and '60s had their roots in his early studies, his contacts with world leaders, his avid attention to detail, as well as his zest for the latest theories on how to solve difficult problems. The diary demonstrates that Kennedy was neither a social activist nor an elitist. It shows him to be far more of an independent thinker than he is sometimes portrayed. His argument that "Mr. Roosevelt has contributed greatly to the end of capitalism in our country" will raise a few eyebrows. His remarks about the terrible conditions in post-war Germany (e.g. "During this winter the situation may be extremely severe. The Colonel thinks that the Russians may be hard pressed. If they are, they undoubtedly will take the food meant for the civilians.") show his deep but very practical compassion and concern for how the people of Europe would pick up their lives and rebuild the economy.

I was hired by Senator John F. Kennedy in 1959 and worked for him as a research assistant in preparation for his 1960 campaign. I was politically naive and undereducated for the job, but survived by hard work. My responsibilities were with his Academic Advisory Committee, which helped gather ideas on foreign policy, defense, economic problems, and all manner of issues from the best and the brightest at Harvard, MIT, and other universities and businesses. Kennedy's wooing of academics was not something new. The man who once contemplated an academic or literary career had reached out to intellectuals all his life; he was hungry for ideas, enjoyed bright people, and dismissed bores. He always wanted facts and not fuzzy thinking. One research task he gave me was to catalogue every statement Khrushchev had made on any public issue. When he needed the results sooner than expected, he called me at home at midnight for a rundown.

When I asked the Senator if I could attend the Democratic Convention in Los Angeles, he hesitated a moment and said he would have to think of something worthwhile for me to do. He then told me I could go to the Convention, but should spend time doing research at the RAND Corporation. I stayed in Santa Monica in July 1960 and met with Albert Wohlestetter, Harry Rowen, and Alain Enthoven, all of whom played a role in shaping the new Administration's defense policy.

The assignment to visit the RAND Corporation was made following a cocktail party I gave for Senator Kennedy's Academic Advisory Committee at an apartment on Beacon Hill in Boston. Many of the thirty-five or so guests would become members of the sub-Cabinet or top White House team. The guests included Professor Walt Rostow of MIT, one of the most prolific and enthusiastic contributors to the group. Professor Rostow urged the Senator to consider his idea for a campaign theme as others tried to edge in to press their thoughts. Professor Rostow persisted and finally JFK put the memo outlining "The New Frontier" into his pocket.

"The New Frontier," soon incorporated into campaign speeches, was more than just a slogan. It was the culmination of long hours of reading by a little boy who was more often sick than well, who spent time alone in school dormitories or hospital rooms reading history and literature and who found solace in ideas and people in all walks of life. Kennedy's reading of history shaped his thinking about world events; he had a firm grasp of geography and from his youth had traveled to places that would be crucial to his performance as President.

The diary is the only known personal record of the future President at this stage of his development. None of the text is found anywhere else in print and none of the stories he filed with the Hearst newspapers duplicate any of the diary material. Except for a dozen handwritten pages, the diary was typed by Kennedy on a small, manual typewriter and gathered into a loose leaf notebook. The few corrections appear in his handwriting. I have not filled in gaps in the text, embellished it, or changed it in any way except for correcting a few obvious typographical errors. For historical accuracy the entire diary is reproduced in facsimile in the back of this book. Brief notes and commentary attempt to explain the background or significance of a given reference or remark, or to supply historical context.

The text of the diary will stand on its own. The writing is significant not only for the story it tells and the glimpses of those world crises JFK would face as President, but for the perception of momentous events by a young man who would shortly be called upon by his father to fill the void left by his brother Joe's death—a burden he undertook just months after his European trip as he began to prepare for his first campaign for Congress. His early thoughts on that campaign are recorded in the later handwritten pages.

As editor of this book and owner of the original document, the question will inevitably be asked—why did you wait until now to publish it? The timing is a matter of personal circumstances. Yet I hope that the delay and the advantage of perspective as well as the opportunity to do the necessary research have helped make the result even more worthwhile. Once I had found the appropriate publisher and Mr. Sidey graciously agreed to write the Introduction, I knew we had the perfect combination for a dignified and fitting tribute to one of the greatest American Presidents.

Deirdre Henderson
October 1995

INTRODUCTION

by Hugh Sidey

■

There was always the aura of adventure about John Kennedy, seemingly beckoned by some distant and restless overture to the stage where the likes of Winston Churchill and Charles de Gaulle and Franklin Roosevelt had stalked history. He coveted the company. He was perpetually enticed by events, exhilarated by maneuver, admiring of brilliance, bemused by human absurdity, angered by failure, and subdued in moments of triumph.

"The great chess game," he used to call it when he was President, this matching of wits with other world leaders, some of whom were principled but many of whom were misshapen by the political pressures of their jobs. When we look back these days we see that while

Kennedy was dangerously naive in some moments even after he entered the White House, there was, as he fitted into this new high-stakes game, a deep core of realism about the world. It echoes out of his past; a past, as this book testifies, that was serious much of the time and was focused on understanding the events and people that drove nations, the preparation of a young man for what was still an ill-defined and distant challenge. Or was it? I choose to think that John Kennedy from almost the day of the war-time death of his older brother, Joe, knew he was joining a caravan of public involvement that would take him to or near the top. "Go for the top," he once told me. "If you aim for second you will end up there."

Kennedy savored the world in remarkable amounts both in personal and political terms, in part because of the accident of birth and the enormous wealth that gave him a magic passport to people and power, in part because of his unrelenting patriarch, who would become infamous for his appetite for money, women, and public success for his numerous offspring, and in part—the biggest part—because of the nature of John Kennedy and the extraordinary impact on him of cataclysmic events during the years in which he matured. Some he watched uncomprehendingly or studied at Harvard (the Great Depression) and some enveloped him (World War II).

I met John Kennedy in 1957 in a Senate elevator,

slouched in a corner, too thin, too rumpled for the world's greatest deliberative body. He was genial but unimpressive, not many months distant from the political whipping that Tennessee's Estes Kefauver had dealt him in order to run as vice presidential nominee with Adlai Stevenson. "Luckiest thing that ever happened to him," his father, Joe Kennedy, once told me without really convincing me. As noted, the Kennedys never entered anything to lose. Six years after that elevator encounter I stood in the concrete parking lot of Dallas' Parkland Memorial Hospital and watched benumbed as Kennedy's body was wheeled down the loading ramp to begin the journey back to Washington and what would be the greatest mourning ritual that the nation had witnessed since the death of Franklin Roosevelt in 1945, just a few weeks before Kennedy began his tour of Europe recorded in this diary. The intense scrutiny of Kennedy the man and President that followed the assassination would reveal some frightening personal lapses but also a leader who had faced difficult challenges both at home and abroad and had charted a reassuring course for the future, even if implementation was lagging.

During those six years I did everything I could to understand this young pretender who had pushed aside the elders of his democratic party, then had confronted and defeated Richard Nixon, the chosen successor by the world's most beloved statesman of that age, Dwight

Eisenhower, and who had jauntily marched into the White House despite his paper-thin electoral victory, judged by many to have been fraudulent. I talked to Kennedy whenever I could—late at night in his Senate office, outside the chamber when he was debating, tossing footballs at his brother Bobby's home, Hickory Hill, in his car between house and Capitol, then, as the campaign began, aboard the family turboprop, the Caroline. Once Kennedy was in the White House he continued to see me with some regularity, whether just to talk in general about events and the people who shaped them or to give his spin on a particular story like the decision to go to the moon, when he sat me in the midst of his space team in the Cabinet room and I listened to the debate between them and the young President.

In those hundreds of conversations I do not recall one that at some point or other did not deal seriously with the problems of the United States he would like to lead (or was leading) and the world he would like to influence. Others have written about Kennedy after hours, the man on the golf course or aboard his yacht, the Honey Fitz, savoring a bowl of fish chowder or dancing to the gay tunes of Lester Lanin's high society orchestra in the White House foyer. That was only rarely my world.

John Kennedy and I were what I like to call the best of the Washington species of professional friends. Our relationship was about our work first and foremost. I met him because I wanted to do stories about him and the subjects like labor reform and running for the Presidency which interested him. He wanted to know me because of the influence around the world of Henry Luce's magazines, at that time the only truly international media. Most of these encounters were focused totally on substantive matters, though usually with some humor and acerbity. Of course, there were frivolous moments, silly asides, lusty references. But after my own modest stint in the army, a pretty good internship among shoeleather reporters, and then a graduate course in political billingsgate while covering Lyndon Johnson, Kennedy's departures from the subject at hand were rather tame affairs. What he displayed for me formed an intriguing stockpile of family lore, world history, and congealing political theology. We did become friends, rather good friends. But there always was the understanding that we viewed each event from a different perspective.

In part this is the reason that I am dissatisfied with some of the modern assessments of him and his Presidency. This is not a denial of his flaws, personal or political, many of which were obscured or ignored in those simpler times. It is to say that there was at the core of his stewardship a continuing and serious effort to steady a difficult world. From my perspective his time both as candidate and President was dominated by hard work, endless meetings and study in policy formation (a tax cut to stimulate growth, civil rights, the war on poverty) and analyzing failure (the Bay of Pigs) when it came, then devising policies that moved beyond the moment. We have in this journal a prelude of sorts to the time of his Presidency, a colorful glimpse of those formative years when undoubtedly his blood ran hot but his mind was considerably cooler and when he moved about the grand stage of international affairs as his father's son, as a blooded veteran of World War II, and as an observer-reporter of the post-war devastation and allied efforts to bring order from the chaos. There are, I have found, many compartments within the souls of men who rise to great power.

Over my four decades of writing about the American Presidency I have been struck at how much the job is shaped by the nature of the man who holds it. That we have a government of laws, not men, is true only as far as it goes, and on some of the modern issues that is not very far. Policy at the top comes out of the heart and mind of the President, or at the very least is tempered by his personality. And his convictions and passions are almost always linked to early impressions gained from family and school and youthful experience. When a politician gains enough prominence to attract attention his main job often is simply armoring himself from the outside assaults and clinging to the basic values and themes that have carried him up to the time. Those political persons who seem too pliable in the shifting electronic currents of this age of the perpetual campaign run grave risks, as George Bush found out when he abandoned his no-new-taxes pledge.

Once in the Presidency there is virtually no time for re-education or the deep introspection that might show a President where he is right or wrong and bring about a true change of mind. Events move too fast. A President may pick up more knowledge about a subject or find an expert aide on whom he can rely, but in most instances when he is alone and faced with a crucial decision he must rely on his intuition, a mixture of natural intelligence, education, and experience. Dwight Eisenhower's genius was engendering trust by the strength of his Kansas common sense. I remained convinced that the strongest impetus for Lyndon Johnson to plunge into the war in Vietnam was what some of us called "the Alamo syndrome," his feeling that somebody should have known and cared about those Texans slaughtered in the old mission in San Antonio. He grew up hearing the story and reading about it.

This book deals with a modest but intriguing new trove of information from Kennedy's young manhood. The personal diary spans the formative meetings of the United Nations in San Francisco, where he had written for Hearst's *Chicago Herald-American* a G.I.'s interpretation of the proceedings, through two months of reporting in Britain, Ireland, France, and Germany in the summer of 1945. He chronicled the political groping during the uncertain days immediately after the war ended in Europe. He saw first-hand the devastation from the masses of modern weapons. He traveled with powerful companions who gave him rare contact with the military and political leaders.

There has been a lot of tortured prose on why Kennedy remains such a revered figure around the world. Looks, money, style, to state the conventional critique. Perhaps some of all of these things weights the conclusion. Yet, I have known in the upper reaches of power many rich persons and many convivial and stylish souls and, by comparison to Kennedy, they all faded to obscurity. I suggest that beneath all the style and glamour Kennedy was basically a serious man on a serious mission. Put another way: his purpose was the essence of his style. All else is empty. And that was and is sensed and respected, if not known in detail, by the millions who heard him and saw him and came later and listened to the stories handed down, and read about him and viewed the scratchy television tapes. Kennedy cared and worked, imperfectly in some instances, but usually with energy and the romantic conviction that he was astride history. That was the greater part of the man I followed from Senate to White House. I am not without my disappointments in John Kennedy as new facts about him have surfaced. More may emerge. But he was in his brief stewardship a man who thought and tried. That part of his legacy deserves a fair viewing.

As one follows John Kennedy through the journal he kept of this unique odyssey, it is plain that he poses worthy ideas about the world and its crop of leaders, worries through (sometimes inexpertly) the fates of competing economic systems; surprising fare from a twenty-eight-year-old, or so it seems in our time half a century later. Yet, by measure of those G.I.'s who carried the brunt of the fighting and dying in World War II while they were still teenagers or in their early twenties, Kennedy was, in the patois of the services, "the old man." He had college and some diplomatic work as an aide to his father under his belt. His senior thesis about Great Britain's unpreparedness for the war had been turned into a best-selling book, *Why England Slept.* And after that he shipped off to the Pacific and commanded PT-109, which was cut in two on an opaque night in 1943 by a Japanese destroyer. Kennedy's heroics in getting the survivors in his crew and himself rescued undoubtedly matured his thoughts about the uses of power, just as some young riflemen on Omaha Beach grew up in minutes.

I know that war—its history, machinery, gamesmanship—was central in much of his political calculation, certainly a natural focus, since the world's struggle to heal itself and establish a secure peace was the biggest story of the time. Power did come out of the barrel of a gun and from those who possessed the most effective weapons. I went in to see Kennedy in his Senate office in the spring of 1960 when he was still struggling to win the democratic nomination. I was questioning him about his knowledge of economics and the New Deal programs which had meant so much to the destitute people of America in the 1930s. "What do you remember about the Great Depression?" I asked. It was one of those times—more would follow—when his absolute candor surprised us both. "I have no first-hand knowledge of the depression," he answered. "My family had one of the great fortunes of the world and it was worth more than ever then. We had bigger houses, more servants, we traveled more. About the only thing that I saw directly was when my father hired some extra gardeners just to give them a job so they could eat. I really did not learn about the depression until I read about it at Harvard." Then, Kennedy took his feet off his desk as if he had cast aside a heavy burden and he leaned forward and said, "My experience was the war. I can tell you about that."

And he did for the better part of an hour as the light faded on Capitol Hill and the corridors in that Old Senate Office Building quieted. He had read the books of great military strategists—Carl Von Clausewitz, Alfred Thayer Mahan, and Basil Henry Liddell Hart—and he wondered if their theories of total violence made sense in the nuclear age. He expressed his contempt for the old military minds, exempting the U.S.'s big three, George Marshall, Douglas MacArthur, and Dwight Eisenhower. "It's amazing that this country picked those men to run things," he said. "Never underestimate democracy." Kennedy chortled over the boasts of those who developed new military technology, claiming the new weapons rarely lived up to their billing—at first. But they were almost always perfected and then stockpiled— and then used. War with all of its modern horror would be his biggest concern if he got to the White House, Kennedy said.

The roots of those thoughts can be found in the diary of the young traveler. Hope blooms among the obvious strengths of free societies but reality tempers euphoria and skepticism is a healthy companion for a would-be writer or politician, a decision not yet fully made by JFK in 1945. It is no less than startling to see his doubts about the effectiveness of the United Nations that soon after the sessions in San Francisco. His worries that the UN would become a haven for bureaucrats and pamphlet writers were all too true, and there is little doubt that watching the UN be created was akin to watching laws and sausage being made; not very reassuring.

By the time Kennedy arrived at the White House he had become such an admirer of Winston Churchill that the fragment in the diary so fulsomely praising Neville Chamberlain and explaining his bending to Hitler's demands is especially intriguing, since it is so out of step with the view, yet unaltered, that Chamberlain was a failed appeaser shoved aside by Churchill, who saw Adolf Hitler's storm coming. Was this some of the defeatist dinner table preaching of old Joe Kennedy, so opposed to the war and so intimidated by the Nazi military machine? Certainly, though I suspect that Kennedy, were he alive today, would take full blame with perhaps a slight wince over the memory of his father's wrong-headedness in that time. I would judge that the sweet-sour relationship which I witnessed later between the two had begun to develop.

The note that "Mr. Roosevelt has contributed greatly to the end of Capitalism in our country" is probably another bit of residue from Old Joe's rantings. It was encouraged by Kennedy's own huge ignorance of economics, an ignorance he confessed to me even while he was in the White House. He just did not know where wealth came from or how it was used. The U.S. was about to embark on half a century of creative and staggeringly successful capitalism, and he missed the signals. But following that thought is a prescient tidbit. Roosevelt, Kennedy asserted, had killed capitalism not through his programs and laws but through "the emphasis he put on rights rather than responsibilities." That is a text that can be found today in the litany of the Republican Speaker of the House, Newt Gingrich. Kennedy became, it seemed to me, a rather happy and sensible combination of liberal compassion and conservative realism.

Kennedy honored his father and respected his achievements in the marketplace. "He's entitled to his views," Kennedy once told me when he was discussing his father. "He made himself." But the son saw a far more complex, crowded, and despairing world than did his father, and sometimes when Old Joe's antics entered the discussion, JFK would roll his eyes and mutter something like, "Different time and different conditions." I think that these journal entries suggest, as much by the things not written as those recorded, that the feelings on policy and leadership by father and son were firmly headed in different directions. Indeed, the book, *Why England Slept,* was a gentle rebuke to the father.

As Kennedy made his way through the post-war debates he picked up on the theme being bruted about by some military leaders that the allies should strike against the Soviet Union immediately, rather than wait for the inevitable clash between the two opposing systems. Kennedy found the idea unacceptable in a democratic system, and, besides, he quite correctly predicted that any clash with the Soviets would be "greatly post-poned," though he did note that events would depend on Soviet self-restraint, an uncertain commodity. By the time that Kennedy had reached the White House he felt that this restraint was running thin. On a despondent evening in the depths of the summer of 1961 he looked across his desk in the Oval Office and told me that he felt a nuclear exchange was inevitable. "Ever since the longbow," he said, "when man had developed new weapons and stockpiled them, somebody has come along and used them. I don't know how we escape it with nuclear weapons."

The Kennedy journal is about war, its possibility or its aftermath in one form or another. Indeed, Kennedy's life was about war almost from the time he began to understand such things. The rise of fascism made the headlines in his home as a child. He puttered around Europe in 1937 on a trip with his friend Lem Billings, whose restrained budget required that the two of them put up in youth hostels, which Kennedy later told me were terrible—jammed with arrogant, smelly Germans. The self-acclaimed master race was marching, and even a twenty-year-old student knew it. Yet, Billings related to me once as we waited through a six-hour delay on the Washington–New York shuttle, Kennedy was fascinated with Hitler and the Hitler youth, young people with a purpose in an otherwise despairing world.

By twenty-eight Kennedy had been in combat and at the time of his journal was picking his way through the debris of World War II, both material and human. It was gritty fare day after day. It made its mark. If I had to single out one element in Kennedy's life that more than anything else influenced his later leadership it would be a horror of war, a total revulsion over the terrible toll that modern war had taken on individuals, nations and societies, and the even worse prospects in the nuclear age as noted earlier. It ran even deeper than his considerable public rhetoric on the issue.

In his travel diary Kennedy writes about the fact that the duchess of Devonshire, whom he was visiting, told him that of seventy-five young men she had known in 1914, seventy were killed in WWI. Stories of death were constant companions on his journey. He had gone on this visit to the English country estate, Compton Place, in Eastbourne, the home of the duke and duchess, with his sister Kathleen Kennedy, who had married Lord Hartington, the son of the duke and duchess. Lord Hartington was killed in battle in 1944. Kennedy mentions Churchill's book, *World Crisis*, which he had read years before, and in it are the chronicles of the terrible slaughter on the Western Front and how the loss of that generation of young men had its effect on British policy. JFK makes yet another rationalization for Prime Ministers Neville Chamberlain and Stanley Baldwin, writing that they "could not bring themselves to subject the young men of Britain to the same horrible slaughter again." In fact, the slaughter worldwide was even greater in the second war, though it took different forms. It is perhaps of limited significance but certainly a coincidence of interest that Speaker Gingrich today rates as one of the most grimly moving experiences of his youth a visit to Verdun, one of WWI's most notable scenes of aimless butchery, where song birds still do not sing.

When Kennedy began to crank up his Presidential campaign I listened somewhat bemused to his private criticisms of Ike. By today's standards they were rather mild and almost always directed vaguely at the Eisenhower Administration rather than the man. With good reason, it turns out. His journal shows two entries on the General, both very complimentary not only for his popularity with Europeans but also for his grasp of the situation in Germany after the war. Kennedy always had high regard for Eisenhower the soldier, even in his moments of political complaining. Humbly mindful of his campaign attacks that Ike had allowed a missile gap and had been indifferent to urban and environmental problems, Kennedy would have to go hat in hand to the retired President for a little bolstering after Kennedy had botched the Bay of Pigs. His original eye on Ike was true.

In his diary, Kennedy seems to be tiptoeing up to the

idea of an atomic bomb, though it was still under secret development when he made that notation. Given the power circle in which he moved he may have had a hint of the weapon being readied for Japan. In the very first entry of his journal there is a paragraph speculating that the U.S. clash (with the Soviets) might be "finally and indefinitely postponed" because of the development of a weapon "so horrible that it will truthfully mean the abolishment of all the nations employing it." A widening group of military and political officials was very much aware of the Manhattan Project by then and it would have been easy for Kennedy to have picked up an alert. At the least he discerned the Soviet brutishness, the dark clouds that would turn into the cold war and the need for allied arsenals to face the challenge.

I think that his encounter with Soviet President Nikita Khrushchev at the Vienna summit in June 1961 dispelled the last vestiges of the terrible weapon theory. Home from that rather grim encounter, Kennedy flew to Palm Beach to rest his painful back, injured when he planted a tree in Canada before his journey abroad. I went to Florida at *Life* magazine's request to talk to him about what had really taken place in his meetings with Khrushchev, and to get his close-in feeling about the Soviet Boss.

"I've never known anyone in politics like him," Kennedy began, after we had had a daiquiri or two and been soothed by Frank Sinatra records. He explained that on every other level when he had been involved in political confrontation that would bring mutual suffering or tragedy if not resolved, the protagonists had agreed to compromise. "There was no area of accommodation with him," Kennedy said. He had brought a model of the USS Constitution as a gift for Khrushchev, and it was in the center of the table near the end of the summit. Kennedy pointed out that each shot from the cannons of the ship only carried half a mile and could kill at best only a few people. But in the first exchange of nuclear weapons, he and Khrushchev could destroy seventy million people. "We can't let that happen," Kennedy implored. As he recalled, he looked directly at Khrushchev and got a blank stare, perhaps the hint of a shrug. It was almost a "so what." The moment was deeply troubling to the President and I believe that black mood grew through the summer of 1961 as the Soviets began to put pressure on Berlin and then erected first the barrier, then the Berlin Wall.

It was in this period that I went to see Bobby Kennedy in his Attorney General's office. We were talking about the President's melancholia, and he added his own chapter. He had never seen his brother cry before, he said. But one evening that summer when John Kennedy was seated on his bed and talking about the threat of war, he got tears in his eyes. He had looked up at his brother and said, "It doesn't matter about you and me and adults so much, Bobby. We've lived some good years. What is so horrible is to think of the children who have never had a chance who would be killed in such a war." His hope that science would render war unthinkable plainly was forgotten. In the longer run, however, his point has had some validity, as we have seen. Nuclear war on a grand scale seems more remote than ever.

The Kennedy travel diary is far from a reporter's notebook. For one thing there are too many polished and completed sentences. Nor is there any of the personal shorthand that journalists usually devise for themselves as they go on their hurried rounds. These are for the most part reflective and literate entries. Kennedy may have had the notion that he might gather his material and expand it into a book once he was done with his journey and could collect all his thoughts. It would be a natural step into a world of writing and commentary on world affairs. I suspect the example of the young Churchill may have lurked somewhere in the back of Kennedy's mind. He never hinted to me that he had ever held ambitions of being a plain reporter, rushing to conferences and battlefields and filing stories from hotel rooms or foxholes. He did tell me once that he had been a great admirer of *Fortune* magazine and its writers and had thought he might want to start some kind of writing career on that publication. I suspect that he was influenced by his teacher and friend, Harvard's John Kennedy Galbraith, who wrote for *Fortune* early in his career and generously credited that experience with enriching his style, a style that would delight President John Kennedy in Galbraith's iconoclastic reports from India, where he was ambassador during The New Frontier.

Kennedy shows in his diary that he has the instincts of a good journalist; the unflagging curiosity, the eyes, the ears. He is in the salons and country homes of too many dukes and lords and the airplanes of too many VIP's for my taste, but that was where the political power struggle was being waged in those days. It also was about the only way a novice journalist could get around and gain entry to the authorities and particularly the Potsdam Conference, the most critical power meeting of the moment. He saw and recorded detail; Hitler's scorched bunker, the daubs of lipstick on some of the German women trying to rise from the gray rubble around them, the difference between the "fat and rosy" folks in the country around Bremen and the "anemic, shocked" Berliners. Kennedy never lost that art of gathering information, in fact, kept improving it. Those skills of observation so necessary to good writers are equally vital to good politicians.

I remember vividly in that Palm Beach session with Kennedy following the Vienna Summit how he seemed to have a camera eye for each scene in which he played.

I asked him to give me an intimate portrait of Khrushchev. He did, and with relish. One would think any President would have a mental printout fresh in his mind after such an event. I would learn that is not always the case. Kennedy took note of Khrushchev's bright, shifting eyes, the quick wit, the clunky gray suit that seemed made in a factory, the peasant vitality in his hand gestures, the peace medal that hung from his lapel, the shadow of fear in his eyes, not about military confrontation, but about not being able to feed his people. Kennedy's mental picture was, to a large degree, that of a writer.

Kennedy's publicly celebrated love of the written word was one of the novelties of his Presidency. It was an extension of his early interest in writing. Some have suggested that he gained his passion for books when he spent weeks in various hospitals in his school years. But obviously he had the kind of intelligence that made him from the start a rapid reader. When Evelyn Wood devised her speed reading course Kennedy, along with other members of his family, signed up. He took a few sessions but, according to Ms. Wood later, dropped out when it was apparent he was beyond the instruction.

I was involved in the somewhat random ritual of deciding that he read 1,200 words a minute, about four times the normal speed of those days. I had become fascinated by the fact that the business of A. T. Schrot,

owner of the Cosmopolitan newsstand on Washington's
15th Street just a block from the White House, had gone
up some 400 percent after Kennedy moved into the Oval
Office. There were other stories about Kennedy swiping
newspapers and rummaging for magazines and most of
them turned out to be true. Kennedy devoured five
newspapers in the morning to start things off, then
grazed through another half dozen during the day. He
looked over and sampled what he wanted from the
nearly twenty magazines he insisted the White House
get. He could consume a novel like Ian Fleming's *From
Russia with Love* in a sitting and a 407-page biography of
Sir Robert Walpole in a single evening. After talking to
Ms. Wood I suggested to the President he probably read
about 800 words a minute. Faster, he suggested to me.
Okay, how fast? A thousand, I offered. He got a big grin
sitting behind his Presidential desk with me, the suppli-
cant, uneasy in front. More, he declared. Okay, let's say
1,200, not a word higher, I replied. Kennedy allowed as
how that was a good estimate. I tried it later on some of
his aides and went back to Ms. Wood who said it was easily within his skills and it seemed to be about as good a
measure as we could get without putting the President
to a reading test, an idea I did not have the courage to
raise.

Though Kennedy was an admirer of style (making
friends with such writers as Teddy White and Bill

Manchester), knowledge was the most prized product when all was said and done. "Roosevelt [Franklin] got most of his ideas from people," Kennedy once told historian James MacGregor Burns. "I get most of mine from reading." Kennedy once asked to see the entire official record from the State Department on the history of Fidel Castro and Communism in Cuba. The document arrived in Kennedy's office in three parts—synopsis, a chronology, and a detailed account. Kennedy took the detailed account.

I suspect that as Kennedy went on this journey he had a good supply of reading material with him. He was an Anglophile and delighted in the romantic accounts of the rise of the British Empire and the great figures on the battlefields or in parliament who made it possible. When he was in the White House and I asked for a list of his ten favorite books,* the top three were about British history. His favorite book—*Melbourne,* by David Cecil—was the story of William Lamb, Prime Minister to Queen Victoria in the glory years of the empire. I still believe that I learned more about Kennedy from that book than any other I read. Here was a society of young, wealthy aristocrats who devoted themselves honorably and tirelessly to service to their queen and empire—and on their weekends to themselves and their pleasures.

---

* this list is reproduced in Appendix A, p. 119.

Kennedy's low-voltage humor runs through the journal, a characteristic that, if anything, enlarged as he rose in politics. His account of his meeting with the duke of Devonshire has that wry touch. The note that the duke believed he was divinely endowed but very conscious of his obligation, which was "furnishing the people of England with a statesman of mediocre ability but outstanding integrity," is a classic Kennedy chuckle. Warmly wicked. On this trip he traveled among his elders, and there is the feeling of true respect. For the most part he retained that sense of propriety as he matured. When he was President, Time Inc.'s boss, Henry Luce, asked to see him and was granted an appointment. Luce sent him a letter requesting that the President call him "Harry," the preferred name and the one used by all his close friends. Just before the Luce visit I was summoned before the President and he asked me what I called Luce. There was no question in my case. "Mr. Luce." Kennedy suspected as much, he said, and then told me about Luce's request. "What would you do in my place?" he asked. I gave a sigh for being burdened with such a grave protocol question, thought a second or two, replied, "I'd call him Mr. Luce, just like you've done since you were a boy." Kennedy smiled. "I agree," he said. "Mr. Luce he will remain."

Kennedy doted on anecdotes about powerful people, which is one of the reasons he was such a devoted reader of the newsmagazines. Some would say he was a

bit of a gossip. And he was. In his travel diary he col-
lected such items. The stories about Eisenhower and
Field Marshal Bernard Montgomery do, as Kennedy
notes, show the contrasting styles of the two war leaders:
Ike still awed that a Kansas boy should be in his position,
Montgomery comfortably convinced of his own superior abilities.

The one solid laugh in the journal is about the foibles
of the rich and powerful, another story passed on to
him by the duke of Devonshire. It seemed that Lady
Violet Bonham-Carter, daughter of Herbert Asquith, a
former Prime Minister, had a habit of leaning her face
closer and closer to those with whom she was talking. At
a dinner party, Alfred Duff-Cooper, ambassador to
France, speared a potato and stuffed it into her mouth,
saying, "Excuse me, I thought it was mine." I can hear
Kennedy giving that low chortle over such a gem. Much
too good an item to leave out of his record. As President
he used to press me for stories I might have gleaned
about the New York–Washington power circle. "How's
Lucie?" he once asked. I was totally baffled. I thought he
was talking about a woman. "Lucie," he insisted. "Henry
Luce. What is he doing these days?"

The amount of the journal which Kennedy devoted
to Ireland is certainly out of proportion to the importance of the problem to the rest of the world at that
moment. He touches on all the post-war Irish doubts

and political turmoil and deals at length with the background and personality of Prime Minister Eamon DeValera, who was bitterly criticized for maintaining strict neutrality during WWII. The Irish visit was, in Kennedy's case, an exercise of the heart. He was rooted there forever. I saw it years later, just a few months before his death. After his triumphant tour of the Berlin Wall and his famous "Ich bin ein Berliner" speech, he flew to Ireland and a bath of pure nostalgia.

DeValera was still about, proud, still erect, though almost blind. At Arbor Hill in Dublin Kennedy laid a wreath on the grave of the fourteen executed leaders of the 1916 uprising. DeValera, who stood beside Kennedy in this remarkable tableau, had been a part of the group but was spared execution because he was relatively unknown then, as Kennedy had written in his youthful journal. I recall that the day in 1963 was misty and gray, the sounds of the military bugles mournful. I made a note to myself on how moved Kennedy seemed to be as he stood before what was a rather small, drab monument. The entries in Kennedy's diary explain that day more fully.

Kennedy's difficulties in understanding and appreciating France's Charles de Gaulle apparently began in the summer of 1945. His brief entry on France starts with de Gaulle's unpopularity and goes on to deal with the unpopularity of the United States and even the inferior quality of France's post-war perfume. France is a difficult woman. Some of those sentiments seemed to echo right down to Kennedy's White House. De Gaulle's haughty independence—particularly his desire to leave NATO and establish an independent nuclear force—frustrated Kennedy in 1961. Kennedy could not convince de Gaulle that if the Soviet Union attacked the western allies, the U.S. would use nuclear weapons. Kennedy's conclusions both in 1945 and 1961 were to leave de Gaulle and his France alone and pass on to other more important things.

Germany was the logical focus of the summer's travel in 1945. The Potsdam Conference was in full swing. Kennedy was traveling with family friend, James Forrestal, the New York banker turned Secretary of the Navy. There is almost a different tone in the section of Kennedy's journal on Germany. Kennedy is going about a somber business, the complete observer-reporter. His senses are sharpened as he watches the land from Forrestal's C-54 and sees the contrast between the peaceful countryside and the ravaged city centers. On the ground he scans the troops on duty, listens to the stories of Russian looting and raping. He finds the stench— "sweet and sickish from dead bodies"—to be overwhelming on some Berlin streets. Kennedy descends into Hitler's scorched bunker and passes along in his journal the persistent rumors that Hitler may still be alive.

Kennedy then was probably as well informed as many journalists and politicians who were crowding into the defeated Germany. But he was terribly in error about the fate of Berlin. "If Germany remains divided into four administrative units as she is now, Berlin will remain a ruined and unproductive city." At this writing I can still hear the roar of the gigantic crowds in a rebuilt, wealthy (though scared) West Berlin in 1963 and see Kennedy in his open car with arms raised in salute to the Berliners. And I can hear him shout at the Soviet doubters, "Lass' sie nach Berlin kommen." Let them come to Berlin. One would hope that if Kennedy were around today he would get a great and gratifying laugh from being so wrong.

Kennedy's German report is somewhat of a mishmash of big politics and bits and pieces that float by him as he tours with Forrestal. All and all it is a competent job of reporting, capturing the chaos that he sees and feels. A profile of a German woman, twenty-two, is an emotional passage about her life and disillusionment under the Nazis and her fierce demonstration to keep the Soviets from raping her. Kennedy pokes into schools and factories, military governments, food distribution and production. Kennedy in his journal does not shy away from figures. After a day talking to Navy officials in Bremen he sizes up the specifications of the German E Boat, the equivalent of his old PT-109, and decides the

German craft was "far superior to our PT boat." In Frankfurt Kennedy sees the underground salt mine with the millions in looted gold, silver, and securities. Then he is on to Berchtesgaden and a look at Hitler's bombed-out mountain chalet and then an ascent to Hitler's Eagle's Nest among the mountain peaks.

The final entry in Kennedy's journal is the most mystifying. He writes that after visiting these two places one could easily understand "how within a few years Hitler will emerge from the hatred that surrounds him now as one of the most significant figures who ever lived." His choice of words is careful—significant, not greatest—suggesting he was in some manner trying to view the scene with cosmic detachment, perhaps as a historian. There is a misty quality about these lines that makes them seem removed from the squalor nearby. Is Kennedy just drifting and dreaming? Whatever, the judgment is bizarre. Had he not heard of the death chambers yet? It is hard to believe. Perhaps Kennedy was just not thinking or writing clearly, or writing to himself in some mysterious way for future reference. Reporters can take such license in their private pages. Yet, Kennedy's final journal line, "He [Hitler] had in him the stuff of which Legends are made," while certainly true, gives no hint that Kennedy sees that the legend is one of a monster. In my time around Kennedy I never heard anything like this.

I suspect that the world of desperation and deadly scheming that Kennedy saw on this trip helped build his appetite for stories of espionage and intrigue which so titillated him as President. In a way the cold war and its dangers appealed to Kennedy. Ian Fleming credited Kennedy's listing of *From Russia with Love* as a favorite book as the bit of publicity that pushed the James Bond series to astronomical success. CIA Director Allen Dulles told me of conversations with Kennedy in which he told the President he was experimenting with some of the gadgetry described in the fictional Bond adventures, such as the tiny radio beeper that could be attached to the underside of an escape car. Kennedy, according to Dulles, was captivated and wanted to know more.

Kennedy once told me that Germany's Chancellor Konrad Adenauer had warned him of spies who carried an odorless, untraceable chemical that if sprayed in anyone's face killed them within minutes. And at that Palm Beach dinner following the Vienna Summit when Kennedy was describing Khrushchev, he took time out to inform me that he had been told the Soviets had sent, part by part through diplomatic pouches, a small atomic weapon, which was assembled on the top floor of their Washington embassy. They would detonate it if the Soviet–American crisis got bad enough, he declared. I was unbelieving and said so. Kennedy got rather stern. "That's what they tell me," he insisted. "Do you know something I don't?" The exchange ended with a mutual smile. I am still not a believer but I have the strange feeling that Kennedy wanted to be.

John F. Kennedy

European
Diary

Summer 1945

Saturday the ———

"War is fatal to a democracy of ...

The war has been won — we without
... our ... & the ... of the enemy
But it is still a question whether we shall ...
... at our own homes. We have been
gravely weakened by this war — ...
... has done a ... to ... that ...
... the loss of many ... hundred thousand
young men ... ...
the clash of ... or ... ...

... the challenge of the ... war
year. We must ... for great ...
... of the ... year ... ... &
our ... than we have ... done on the
past

Salana de Wolfgang(?) once wrote

"War is fatal to democracy if beaten et[c?].

This war has been won—we won't lose our liberty at the hands of the enemy

But it is still a question whether we shall have it at our own terms.(?) We have been gravely weakened by this war—our values(?) have been changed as never before   we have suffered the loss of nearly 8 hundred thousand young men—many of whom might become (?) the leadership we will so desperately need

To meet the challenges of the post war years we must show far greater concern for the (?) (?) (?) (?) and our country than we have ever shown in the past

THE SAN FRANCISCO
CONFERENCE

July 10, 1945*

The Conference at San Francisco suffered from inadequate preparation and lack of fundamental agreement among the Big Three; from an unfortunate Press which praised it beyond all limit at its commencement which paved the way for subsequent disillusionment both in England and in this country.

The finished Charter is a product of these weaknesses — but it is also the product of the hope, and even more, the realization that humanity can ill afford another war.

In practice, I doubt that it will prove effective in the sense of its elaborate mechanics being frequently

* Though dated July 10, 1945, this is the first entry in the diary. From the next entry, June 21, 1945, the diary proceeds chronologically. Whether the date here is correct in unknown.

employed or vitally decisive in determining war or peace.

It is, however, a bridge between Russia and the Western world and makes possible discussion and a personal relationship which can do much to ease mutual suspicion.

The great danger is that the mechanism will not be employed; the trusteeship machinery will be used for only unimportant islands; the Social and Economic Body of the General Assembly will merely issue significant pamphlets on world conditions — significant in their content but not in their effect. And lastly, in far greater importance, because none of the larger countries will be willing, in the final analysis, to put the decision of war or peace in the hands of a delegate to a council, the Security Council will wither on the vine.

Instead, the Big Three meetings will continue to be called to settle ticklish problems — which is good for temporary emergencies but a poor solution over long periods of time for it arouses distrust through the world and does not contribute to building a firm foundation for peace based on principle — but rather makes a virtue of expediency.

As to the future, I do not agree with those people who advocate war now with the Russians on the argument "Eventually, why not now?" Fortunately, or unfortunately, depending on how you view it, democracies have to go through a gradual disillusionment in their hopes of peace; war must be shown to be the only alternative to preserve their independence — or at least they must believe this to be true.

This was the great contribution of Neville Chamberlain who by giving Hitler every possible opportunity, shaming himself and indeed England to the world, finally convinced not only the Empire but even the United States that Germany was truly headed down the road to war. He made the way easy for his successor, Mr. Churchill, for he paved the eventual way for the entry of the United States into World War II. They were an admirable team — Mr. Churchill and Mr. Chamberlain — in securing our declaration, and of the two, I think that the latter did the most. He is given scant credit for it, particularly by the English people themselves, but perhaps history will be more generous.

I think that the clash with Russia will be greatly postponed. It will come perhaps, as its avoidance depends chiefly on the extent of Russia's self-restraint, and that is a quality of which powerful nations have a limited quantity.

The clash may be finally and indefinitely postponed by the eventual discovery of a weapon so horrible that it will truthfully mean the abolishment of all the nations employing it. Thus Science, which has contributed so much to the horrors of war, will still be the means of bringing it to an end.

If this is not done, the clash will take place — probably involving first the British, perhaps in Persia, for the British are in great danger of sinking to a second-class power under the onslaught of Communism both in Asia and Europe. And they may prefer to fight rather than face it.

THE BRITISH
ELECTION

June 21, 1945

Tonight it looks like Labor and a good thing it will be for the cause of free enterprise. The problems are so large that it is right that Labor, which has been nipping at the heels of private enterprise in England for the last twenty-five years, should be faced with the responsibility of making good on its promises.

D— maintains that free enterprise is the losing cause. Capitalism is on the way out — although many Englishmen feel that this is not applicable to England with its great democratic tradition and dislike of interference with the individual.

I should think that they might be right in prosperous times, but when times go bad, as they must inevitably, it will be then that controls will be clamped on — and then the only question will be the extent to which they are tightened.

Socialism is inefficient; I will never believe differently, but you can feed people in a socialistic state, and that may be what will insure its eventual success.

Mr. Roosevelt has contributed greatly to the end of Capitalism in our own country, although he would probably argue the point at some length. He has done this, not through the laws which he sponsored or were passed during his Presidency, but rather through the emphasis he put on rights rather than responsibilities — through promises like, for example, his glib and completely impossible campaign promise of 1944 of 60,000,000 jobs.

He must have known that it was an impossibility to ever implement this promise, and it will hang as a sword over the head of a Capitalistic system — a system that will be discredited by its inability to make that promise good.

June 29, 1945

Kathleen and I went down this afternoon to Eastbourne in southern England to Compton Place. Eastbourne is a small village and Compton Place is in the center of it, though for its quietness it might be in the middle of a large forest.

Its owner, the Duke of Devonshire, is an eighteenth-century story book Duke in his beliefs — if not in his appearance. He believes in the Divine Right of Dukes, and in fairness, he is fully conscious of his obligations — most of which consist of furnishing the people of England with a statesman of mediocre ability but outstanding integrity.

David Ormsby-Gore maintains that in providing the

latter service the Aristocracy, especially the country squires, really earn their sometimes extremely comfortable keep.

The Duke was a good friend of Neville Chamberlain. He went on several fishing trips with him, but he said that he could never understand Chamberlain's idea of confiscating part of his land providing some "compensation" was made by the State. "But," said the Duke, "what compensation can there be by handing over my property to a middle-class official who can't administer it half as well." And there you have the social philosophy of Edward, tenth Duke of Devonshire.

He had a number of interesting stories. One was about Lady Violet Bonham-Carter, daughter of Herbert Asquith, former Prime Minister.

Lady Violet had a great habit of bringing her face gradually closer and closer to the subject of her conversation until finally only several inches separated her from the recipient of her remarks. Duff-Cooper, Ambassador to France, finally became so infuriated with this habit that, at a dinner party, he suddenly picked up a potato with his fork and dashed it into her mouth saying, "Excuse me, I thought it was mine."

He was interesting on the subject of Nepal — an independent country from which the famous Ghurka warriors come. Great Britain was unable to conquer this principality so since the nineteenth-century conquest they have lived in peace with the Maharaja in close alliance.

The Ghurka soldier — crack troops — are mercenaries, who, being Moslems and therefore unable to cross the sea, have to go through an elaborate purification process before being allowed to enter their country after their tour of duty is complete.

Part of this purification process consists of bathing in cow urine and eating some cow manure.

As far as India on the whole, the Duke (Under-Secretary of State for Colonies) sees little hope for the future — due to the terrific hostility of the Moslems and the Hindu's on the one hand and the completely mystic and debasing position of the 30 million "Untouchables" on the other. It is a poor foundation on which to build a democracy.

He admits, however, that England would also suffer if she were cut off completely from India, but the commercial ties are steadily becoming weakened by the growth of Indian heavy industry and the influx of the goods of other countries.

In the Levant, France had been consistently warned. It was France's traditional policy of domination of this part of the middle East which was carried out at a time when French prestige and power was too weak to successfully carry it through.

Although the Duke is an anachronism with hardly the adaptability necessary to meet the changing tides of present day, he does have great integrity and lives simply with simple pleasures. He has a high sense of noblesse oblige, and it comes sincerely for him. He believes that Labor will win an overwhelming victory. He is the only Conservative that I have heard state this view.

His wife, grand-daughter of Lord Salisbury, Prime Minister of England, is a woman of intense personal charm and complete selflessness.......................

June 30, 1945

General Eisenhower has taken a great hold on the hearts of all the British people. A typical story they tell: At the fall of Tunis in Africa back in 1943, a parade was held of all the forces that had brought the African campaign to a successful conclusion.

As the crack Eighth Army filed past, the Desert Rats, the Highland Division, the South Africans — all experienced and excellent troops — Eisenhower, as the supreme Commanding Officer, took the salute. He was heard to say after the Eighth had marched past, "To think that I, a boy from Abilene, Kansas, am the Commander of troops like those!" He never lost that humble way and therefore easily won the hearts of those with whom he worked.

Montgomery, on the other hand, while holding a unique position himself, won it the other way. Shortly before he went to take over the Eighth Army in the desert, Montgomery was heard to say, "A military career is a hard one — you win a battle and you are a hero — you lose one and you are disgraced."

The man with whom he talked said, "Cheer up, General, you should do well — you have good troops and fine equipment." "But," said Montgomery with some surprise, "I wasn't talking about myself, I was thinking of Rommel."

The Duchess said that the slaughter in the first war was extreme. Of seventy-five young men that she had known in 1914, seventy were killed in the war.

Churchill in his book "World Crisis" brings out the same point — the terrific slaughter of the field officers of the British army — two or three times higher than the Germans. They were always on the defensive in the dark days of '15, '16, and '17, and they paid most heavily.

The British lost one million of a population of forty million; the French, one million five hundred thousand of a population of thirty-eight million; and the Germans, one million five hundred thousand of a population of seventy million.

This tremendous slaughter had its effect on British policy in the 30's when Chamberlain and Baldwin could not bring themselves to subject the young men of Britain to the same horrible slaughter again.

NOTE:

Churchill in his book "The Crisis" brings home with great force the amazing confidence and dependence that the British have put in their fleet as their number one line of defense.

July 1, 1945

I had dinner with William Douglas-Home, former Captain in the British army, third son of Earl of Home, cashiered and sentenced to a year in jail for refusal to fire on _____ at LeHavre.

He is quite confident that his day will come after his disgrace has passed, and he quotes Lord Beaverbrook to the effect that some day he will be Prime Minister to England. Like Disraeli he is extremely confident.

He feels that by insisting on the doctrine of "Unconditional Surrender" instead of allowing Germany and Russia both to remain of equal strength, we made it possible for Russia to obtain that very dominance that we fought Germany to prevent her having.

He feels that we had a great opportunity for a balance of power policy.

For my own part, I think that only time can tell whether he was right, but I doubt that William Home will ever meet much success because people distrust those who go against convention. And furthermore, prowess in war is still deeply respected. The day of the conscientious objector is not yet at hand.

July 2, 1945

The great danger in movements to the Left is that the protagonists of the movement are so wrapped up with the end that the means becomes secondary and things like opposition have to be dispensed with as they obstruct the common good.

When one sees the iron hand with which the Trade Unions are governed, the whips cracked, the obligatory fee of the Trade Union's Political representatives in Parliament, you wonder about the liberalism of the Left. They must be most careful. To maintain Dictatorships of the Left or Right are equally abhorrent no matter what their doctrine or how great their efficiency.

July 3, 1945

I attended a political rally this evening at which Professor Harold Laski, Chairman of the Executive Council of the Labor Party and erstwhile Professor at the London School of Economics, spoke. He spoke with great venom and bitterness, and at the conclusion when asked if it were true that he wrote a letter to Mr. Attlee requesting him to resign as head of the Labor Party, he replied with asperity that it was "none of their business."

Odd this strain that runs through these radicals of the Left. It is that spirit which builds dictatorships as has been shown in Russia. I wonder whether a dictatorship of the Left could ever get control in England, a country with such a great democratic tradition. The next few years will answer that question.

These Leftists are filled with bitterness, and I am not sure how deeply the tradition of tolerance in England is ingrained in these bitter and discontented spirits. I think that unquestionably, from my talk with Laski, that he and others like him smart not so much from the economic inequality but from the social.

In speaking of Boston, he said, "Boston is a state of mind — and as a Jew, he could understand what it is to be an Irishman in Boston." That last remark reveals the fundamental, activating force of Mr. Laski's life — a powerful spirit doomed to an inferior position because of his race — a position that all his economic and intellectual superiority cannot raise him out of.

July 24, 1945

I left England yesterday to come to Ireland. World attention has been turned again to Mr. DeValera due to his recent remark in the "Irish Dail" that Ireland was a Republic. I stayed with Mr. David Gray, the American Minister to Ireland.

Mr. Gray's opinion of DeValera was that he was sincere, incorruptible, also a paranoiac and a lunatic. His premise is that the partition of Ireland is indefensible, and once this thesis is accepted, all else in its policy is consistent. He believed Germany was going to win. He kept strict neutrality even towards the simplest United States demand.

Mr. Gray admits that Mr. DeValera was not any more

friendly to the Germans than he was to us. He does not think German submarines were aided from Ireland, at least with the knowledge of Mr. DeValera, although there were many German sympathizers.

He quoted the Cardinal in 1940 as having said that "he would take Germany as soon as England." The Cardinal believes that Ireland was created by God — a single island and people, and partition is therefore an offense to God. Gray says the island was maintained by the British during the war — gasoline, shoes, and coal — all were British.

He feels that the Civil War of 1921 was caused by the pride of DeValera. DeValera's constitutional proposals were very similar to those favored by President Cosgrave, Michael Dillon, and a majority of the "Dail." Yet, he split the country over the issue.

DeValera has a unique political machine. Only one member of his caucus ever voted against him. He has a way of bringing the national issue into every question. He joined neutrality in this war with the independence of Ireland. Either you were for neutrality and against partition or if you were against neutrality you were for partition. As a Parliament and political boss he is unique.

Gray admits he only caught DeValera once in the "Dail." DeValera had made the statement that Ireland had been completely blocked by Germany and England. Mr. Gray proved him wrong. Gray feels that Ireland should not attempt to become self-sufficient but rather should become a highly intensified agricultural country.

Gray states that DeValera expected America and England to follow out again at the end of this war as they did at the end of the last war. If this had happened, he would have been proved right. He did not figure on Russia, which is now holding these two countries together.

Churchill's speech at the end of the war, in which he attacked DeValera, was extraordinarily indiscreet — made things much more difficult for Gray and pulled DeValera out of a hole.

James Dillon, in opposition to DeValera, believes that far more could have been gotten by friendship with Britain and by building mutual confidence. He feels that DeValera is farther from their partition than when he started.

Gray said that the Irish President's Secretary paid a courtesy call on the German Legation at the time of Hitler's death. He did not pay a call on the American Legation at the time of Roosevelt's death. Now there is a new President but O'Reilly, the Secretary, has been kept on at the insistence of DeValera.

Gray says that of the 200,000 people who left Ireland

for England, only 30,000 joined the British army in this war. In the first war 50,000 were killed and 250,000 in service.

(End of talk with Gray)

DE VALERA

July 25, 1945

DeValera was born in New York, the son of a Spanish father and Irish mother. He took part in Sir Roger de Casement's Rebellion in 1916, which through lack of German help was unsuccessful. The Revolutionists seized the city for a week but were finally overpowered by the British.

At this time they had little public support as the British had successfully imposed a complete blackout on news.

The leaders were jailed, and in order to impress the populace, the British commenced to shoot their leaders — one or two a day. DeValera was comparatively unknown and therefore near the end of the list, and because public indignation had come to a fever pitch in America and Ireland due to the daily executions, the British reprieved DeValera and removed him to an English jail.

There he was confined until he finally arranged his escape. He took some wax from the altar where he was serving Mass, made an impression of a key, and had one of his companions draw a Christmas card showing a drunk coming home from a Christmas party trying to put a very large key into a very small key hole. Another drawing showed another drunk coming home trying to put a very small key into a very large key hole. This card was sent to his friends in Ireland where it lay around for several months before one day someone picked it up and realized what it was.

Michael Collins, the great Irish hero, arranged for keys to be sent to DeValera in jail in a cake and went to England himself to aid the escape. One of the keys broke but at the last minute Mr. DeValera was successful in breaking out.

He was met by Collins and smuggled across to Ireland and thence to the United States where he argued sympathy for Ireland's fight for freedom at the end of the war against the Black and Tans. He returned to Ireland and broke with Collins and Cosgrave over their acceptance of a treaty with Great Britain. Though Collins was killed,

DeValera was defeated, and since that time he has fought politically in the "Dail" the same battle that he fought militarily in the field — a battle to end partition, a battle against Great Britain.

He came to power eventually in 1932 over the question of annuities — the money that the Irish were paying to the British for the land that had been taken from the landlords and given to the Irish peasants.

Mr. DeValera opposed these payments, and the peasants who would have had to pay 50 per cent of this sum supported him strongly because it pleased both their pocketbook and their independent capitalistic spirit.

England retaliated by setting a tariff on every head of cattle shipped to England. This tariff had to be paid by Ireland to keep its market. This was a great financial loss to Eire, and the matter was finally settled after a long economic war by an outright payment of $10,000,000 cash. This, combined by the money paid by tariff, came to a greater amount than the annuities had been in the first place.

Because of DeValera's appeal to nationalism and his mystic hold on the hearts of the people and his practical politics, he did not lose control.

Ireland was in a poor condition at the end of this economic war as nearly 200,000 cows were slaughtered because of the British tariff.

FINANCE

Ireland receives about $4,000,000 a year from the United States in remittances as she needs about $15,000,000 more to pay for her imports. Her dollar exchange has been given her by England. This put Ireland in a position of independence.

Many Irishmen feel that it is a great mistake to be so closely tied up with the sterling bloc. It is bondage they claim.

England has many weapons with which she could strangle Ireland — a tariff on beef, shutting off her credit, as well as the use of force. England so far has done remarkably in practicing self-restraint, but Gray believes that on its previous form it will probably make some serious error in the future.

(NOTE:)
Sheridan once said, "The quarrel is a very pretty quarrel as it stands; we should only spoil it by trying to explain it."

(NOTE:)
A thought for Irishmen abroad — written by Thomas D'Arcy McGee, a Canadian of Irish birth.

"Our first duty is to the land where we live and have fixed our homes; and where, while we live, we must find the true sphere of our duties. While always ready therefore to say the right word and do the right act for the land of my forefathers, I am bound above all to the land where I reside."

IRELAND

The two chief parties of Ireland are the Fine Gael
(United Ireland Party) and the Fianna Fail — the "soldiers of Ireland Party."

The former is led by General Mulcahy and was organized by William Cosgrave. It is always believed that the
way to end partition is to cooperate with the British —
not fight them.

The Fianna Fail, now the most powerful party in
Ireland, is DeValera's party which came into power in
1930. Both these parties are fighting the same political
battle in the "Dail" that they fought in the Civil War.

What has weakened Cosgrave's party is that DeValera

who has bitterly opposed Great Britain was the party that ended British control of the ports — a concession that Great Britain was unwilling to give Mr. Cosgrave in spite of his sincere desire to cooperate.

This has given DeValera ammunition and has given some substance to his feeling that everything that has ever been gotten by Ireland from England has been given grudgingly and at the end of a long and bitter battle.

Seventy per cent of the Irish population is on the land. This gives the population a very conservative outlook.

When a politician in Ireland speaks of the "Left" he is not referring to its attitude towards national industry but rather its attitude towards the Republic and the ending of partition. The Left is the anti-British group — the Right those in favor of working out a compromise.

DeValera in his efforts to make this island self-sufficient and lessen its dependence on Great Britain has raised the wheat acreage from 20,000 to 200,000 from 1932 to 1944.

This may increase its economic self-sufficiency, but wheat is not a profitable product for misty, rainy Ireland to grow.

IMPRESSION OF BRITISH
ELECTION RESULTS

July 27, 1945

The overwhelming victory of the Left was a surprise to everyone. It is important in assaying this election to decide how much of the victory was due to a "time for a change" vote which would have voted against any government in power, whether Right or Left, and how much was due to real Socialistic strength.

My own opinion is that it was about 40 per cent due to dissatisfaction with conditions over which the government had no great control but from which they must bear responsibility — 20 per cent due to a belief in Socialism as the only solution to the multifarious problems England must face — and the remaining 40 per cent due to a class feeling — i.e.; that it was time "the working man" had a chance.

For too long a time now England has been divided into the two nations as Disraeli called them — the rich and the poor.

The Labor Party will stay in for a long time if the conservative wing of that party — men like Attlee and Bevin remain in office.

But if the radical group like Laski, Shinwell, and Cripps become the dominating influence in the party, there will be a reaction and the Conservatives will come once again to power. In my own opinion Attlee will remain in office for the next year and a half, but if there is much dissatisfaction, which there well may be, he will go; and as a sop to the radical Left wing, Morrison or Bevin will take over.

Labor is laboring under the great disadvantage of having made promises to numerous groups whose aims are completely incompatible. The Conservatives may pick up some of these votes, at least those of the middle class when conditions make it impossible for Labor to implement many of its promises.

SOME FIGURES WHICH
EMPHASIZE BRITAIN'S PROBLEMS

Only by being highly organized by government directives can Britain grow as much as 2/3 of the food necessary to feed her population.

IN 1938:

Britain consumed imports of	858,000,000 pounds
The government made payments overseas of	13,000,000 pounds
	Total
	871,000,000 pounds

Export of merchandise	471,000,000 pounds
Income from overseas investments	200,000,000 pounds
Net shipping earnings	200,000,000 pounds
Misc.	35,000,000 pounds
Revenue	806,000,000 pounds
Deficit	65,000,000 pounds

Total external debt of Great Britain in 1945 is 5,000,000,000 pounds of which the India debt is 1,000,000,000 pounds.

Notes on France

July 28, 1945

People are disappointed with DeGaulle. He has not pleased any group (which may be a sign of fair government) and has made himself extremely unpopular with most. Any movement against DeGaulle will take the form of a swing to the Left — the victory of the Socialists in Britain may accentuate this swing.

Food is hard to get for people in the city because of lack of transportation. This lack of transportation has contributed greatly to the difficulties all throughout Europe.

United States unpopularity is strengthened by the fact that we control most of the rolling stock (railroad, cars, trucks, etc.) and use it to feed and supply our own forces. The French have nothing.

MONETARY:

The Franc is stabilized at 50 to the dollar. This is an artificial rate — the actual ratio is nearer 150 to the dollar. This gives the French a bonus as prices are on the 150 Franc ratio scale and our troops are paid at the 50 to the dollar ratio. Importers into France, of course, have an advantage under this setup, but exporters who are attempting to sell brandies and wines are at a substantial disadvantage.

The French plan for a capital levy is extremely interesting and may prove a precedent for other countries in Europe and eventually throughout the world.

The present plan is for the government to take over 5 per cent of the stock and sell it to the public, keeping the profit for themselves.

This may be done up to 20 per cent.

NOTE:

Perfumes and other luxury goods are no longer of first-class quality. Perfumes are not the musk base of former days. The musk supply, which comes from the East, has been turned off.

GERMANY

July 29, 1945

With Secretary of the Navy Forrestal and others of his party, we left Paris at about three o'clock in the Secretary's C54 plane for Berlin.

In flying over Germany, the small towns and fields looked peaceful, but in the larger cities like Frankfurt the buildings are merely of the sods. All the centers of the big cities are of the same ash gray color from the air — the color of churned up and powdered stone and brick. Railroad centers are especially badly hit, but the harvest seems to be reasonably good and the fields appear as though they were being worked fully.

At the field at Berlin where we arrived, Prime Minister Attlee came in just ahead of us. There was a large crowd, and he inspected the same Guard of Honor which Prime Minister had inspected only a few days before. We drove immediately to Potsdam through miles of Russian soldiers. They were stationed on both sides of the road at about 40 yard intervals — green-hatted and green-epauleted — Stalin's personal and picked guard. They looked rugged and tough, unsmiling but with perfect discipline. As the cars drove by, they presented arms.

We stopped in front of the President's house which was in a peaceful Potsdam square untouched by war. It was small but surrounded by our own M.P.'s, evidently influenced by the Russians because they saluted and stood at attention like Marines.

Here, as in all the rest of Germany, the Army discipline was perfect — a far cry from the laxity of Paris. Outside of the President's house were the plain-clothes men of the American Secret Service. They looked big and tough and equally as unsmiling as the Russians.

The Secretary talked to the President for a few minutes, and then we drove to a house on the Kleine Wann See — a beautifully furnished house on a wonderful location along a beautiful lake. It was untouched by bombs, but during the evening as we drove along the lake in a speed boat, many of the houses in this residential section were badly hit.

NOTES:

The Russian Army in Berlin now is the second Russian Army to be in occupation. The first army, which was the fighting army, had been withdrawn by the time we arrived. The Russians gave the first army a 72-hour pass after they had taken the city, and raping and looting was general. What they didn't take, they destroyed. When that army had been withdrawn, the second Russian Army was given the same leave and the same privileges, but since that time the discipline has been better. The Russians have been taking all the able-bodied men and women and shipping them away. Prisoners that we released are taken up and sent back to Russia.

All the children under fifteen or women over fifty and old men are dumped into the American zone and thus become an American responsibility.

(FEEDING)

There are approximately 900,000 originally in the American zone. The French have been added to the occupation forces at the expense of the British who now have 200,000 fewer to feed. But it means that the Americans now have 200,000 extra mouths to feed as the Americans are supplying food for the French district.

(NOTE)

There seems to be a general feeling here that the Germans hoped that the German Army would stop fighting in the West and permit the Allies to come in before the Russians. As far as the Russian treatment of the Germans, most admit that it was as bad as the propaganda had told them it would be. Raping was general. The Russians stole watches in payment and cameras were second choice. The Russians have recently been paid and they are very free with their money. The standard price for watches brought some Americans over $400. The official rate of exchange is 10 marks to the dollar.

One opinion here is that the Russians are never going to pull out of their zone of occupation but plan to make their part of Germany a Soviet Socialist Republic. The question, therefore, is whether the other three occupying forces can afford to leave their zones. So far, the British seem to be encouraging a German economic revival. (The new British government may change this.)

The French who are in the Rhine area will probably want to continue to take large portions of German production. The United States will probably want to pull out — the present plan is to keep an occupying army of 400,000. If a split among the Big Four develops as far as long-time administrative procedure, it will be serious.

July 29, 1945

Germany will be unable to build and maintain communications, roads, canals, trade, coal, and food. If we don't withdraw and allow them to administer their own affairs, we will be confronted with an extremely difficult administrative problem. Yet, if we pull out, we may leave a political vacuum that the Russians will be only too glad to fill.

IMPRESSIONS OF
BERLIN RUINS

The devastation is complete. Unter der Linden and the streets are relatively clear, but there is not a single building which is not gutted. On some of the streets the stench — sweet and sickish from dead bodies — is overwhelming.

The people all have completely colorless faces — a yellow tinge with pale tan lips. They are all carrying bundles. Where they are going, no one seems to know. I wonder whether they do.

They sleep in cellars. The women will do anything for food. One or two of the women wore lipstick, but most seem to be trying to make themselves as unobtrusive as possible to escape the notice of the Russians.

The Russians were short, stocky, and dour looking. Their features were heavy and their uniforms dirty.

Hitler's Reich Chancellery was a shell. The walls were chipped and scarred by bullets, showing the terrific fight which took place at the time of its fall. Hitler's air-raid shelter was about 120 feet down into the ground — well furnished but completely devastated. The room where Hitler was supposed to have met his death showed scorched walls and traces of fire. There is no complete evidence, however, that the body that was found was Hitler's body. The Russians doubt that he is dead.

TALK WITH COL. HOWLIE, CHIEF OF AMERICAN MILITARY GOVERNMENT IN BERLIN

On our arrival in Berlin, the American group was viewed with profound distrust. The Russians did not let them take over for the first few days using as their excuse — that they had to have time to evacuate. The Col. thinks, however, that it was because they wanted to continue their looting.

The Colonel ordered his staff to move in one morning. When the Russians arrived at their offices, they found the Americans already there. After a few protests, they retired. Now things are working reasonably smoothly.

All decisions have to be unanimous between the four occupying powers. They run the city as a unit — they work disputes over until the decision is unanimous.

Up until now the food for the American zone is delivered by the Americans to the edge of the Russian zone in the West, which extends 200 miles west of Berlin. Then the Russians transport it to Berlin. After August fifteenth, when the bridges and roads are fixed, the United States will bring their food in directly.

The basic ration is 1 ½ pounds a day — approximately 1,200 calories (2,000 considered by the health authorities for normal diets — the ration is only 900 calories in Vienna).

The British ship in about 9,000 tons of coal a day for the city which is used for public utilities and for the services of the occupying forces. During this winter the situation may be extremely severe. The Colonel thinks that the Russians may be hard pressed. If they are, they undoubtedly will take the food meant for the civilians. This may present a problem for us because the Americans cannot feed their civilians better than those in the Russian zone because this would cause an influx from all over Berlin.

The Russians have pretty well plundered the country, have been living off it — and therefore, although they control the food basket of Germany, they may never be able to develop their quota for this winter.

The Russian staff work, according to the Colonel, is sloppy. When they make appointments, they may not keep them. Ordinarily, this is not due to indifference to the Americans but merely because they are home drunk in bed. The Colonel says that Americans have to talk tough and know their facts. He does feel, however, that the suspicion between the Russians and the Americans has lessened since the occupation began.

TALK WITH PIERRE HUSS,
CHIEF OF THE INS BUREAU OF BERLIN

The Russians moved in with such violence at the beginning — stripping factories and raping women — that they alienated the German members of the Communistic Party, which had some strength in the factories.

German Communists protested to Zhukov, who has now moved in another Army, the show army, and the Russians are now allowing political activity though strictly controlled. There are four political parties — all left wing — and the Russians are going to bring back the Paulis Committee from Moscow which they hope may be able to rally the powerful old families. (This looks like a dubious hope to me.)

The Russians are putting it over us as far as political

activity goes — they have opened the schools, they are publishing papers — we have done none of these things. We seem to have no definite policy.

I feel myself that the Russians have a long way to go before they can erase the first terrible impression they made on the Berliners. Therefore, any political activity which is backed directly by Moscow will have great difficulty in meeting much public support among the Germans.

CONVERSATION WITH
A GERMAN GIRL

This girl is about twenty-two, speaks some English, and is a Roman Catholic. She said it was difficult to get to Catholic church after the Nazis came to power, though it was possible. She thought the Germans were going to win the war but the first victories were just "shiny."

She thought the future of Germany is "melancholy." After finishing her secondary school education, she worked for a year doing manual labor. The work was extremely hard. She then returned to the University and as the war got increasingly severe, she went to the western front and worked with a search-light crew. She felt that the war was lost in 1942 when American planes came over.

When the Russians came, she and her two sisters were taken down to the cellar. Her clothes were "taken out" — she gave them all her rings, cried, waved a bottle of wine. Her "face was blue." She demonstrated by swinging a bottle at me. I can quite believe that no Russian would want to rape her. She says the Russians let them go untouched. When the Russians saw the Holy Mother's picture and the Crucifix on the wall, they said, "You must be anti-Nazi if you're a Catholic."

People did not realize what was going on in the concentration camps. In many ways the "SS" were as bad as the Russians. The feeding in Berlin was extremely well organized, even in the most severe blitz.

Her brother was killed on the Eastern front and her fiance is in an Italian prisoner-of-war camp. She feels that Russia and the United States will fight when Russia is ready. They now know that our equipment is far superior.

She feels that that war would be the ruination of Germany which would be the common battleground.

NOTE:

SS was enlarged in 1942 because Himmler wanted to increase his own power. Their brutality was, therefore, diluted by forced recruits.

NOTE:

According to our naval experts, the bombing of Germany was not effective in stopping their production and production increased three-fold during 1942-44.

NOTE:

One of the debatable questions now in Berlin is whether Berlin will ever be built up again into a large city. If Germany remains divided into four administrative units as she is now, Berlin will remain a ruined and unproductive city. In any case, it will be many years before Berlin can clear the wreckage and get the material to rebuild.

BREMEN

July 29, 1945*

Arrived in Bremen from Berlin in the morning. Met at airport by Rear Admiral Robinson, former Commander of the Marblehead. Had lunch and then went to Bremerhaven — a large port on the North Sea which is now filled with many ships including the Europa.

The countryside surrounding Bremen is beautiful and the crops were abundant. Cattle, sheep, and chickens were numerous. (The Dutch and French claim that they were stolen from them.)

The people were fat and rosy, completely unlike the

---

* Though dated July 29, 1945, the previous day's entry, also dated July 29, 1945, indicates that Kennedy left Paris at 3 p.m. for Berlin. He thus could not have "arrived in Bremen from Berlin in the morning [of the 29th]." Please see Notes for further discussion.

anemic, shocked, and frightened Berliners. There was little evidence of war — no bomb damage. This area will do well this year.

The harbor of Bremerhaven was full of captured ships. The Europa was getting up steam as we drove in and should be ready to leave in another month for America to be converted into a troop transport. She still has aboard her old Captain and some of the crew who were with her when she was making her old transatlantic runs. He was captured by the British on a raid on Narvik, was interned in Canada, and repatriated in 1944, and has been on the ship ever since. They may keep him aboard with many of the old engineers, as they are skilled, speak English, and do not seem to have had close Nazi connections.

From there we went to a gigantic new construction intended for a Willow Run type of submarine production, the submarines to be produced at the rate of one every two days. It was over 400 yards long, 100 yards wide, and 70 yards high. The concrete on the roof was 14 feet thick, and although one bomb had pierced it, the roof due to its extremely clever design was nearly intact. They were getting ready to double the thickness of the roof which would have been an architectural and engineering masterpiece when the war ended. Construction is being pushed on this building right up to the war's end.

From there we went to a ship-yard where they were assembling pre-fabricated submarines. The parts were assembled in the South and East and the sections were brought by barges along the canals and assembled here. The bombing had not damaged any of the 24 submarines along the water's edge, although the wreckage was heavy about a quarter of a mile in shore. The British seem to have concentrated and bombed only the machine and tool shops.

Figures were given which showed German submarine production at about one a day. 11,000 were launched from 1939 to 1945, and Forrestal said 600 had been sunk.

These submarines were all equipped with the Schozzle breathing device which enabled them to stay under water for long periods. One submarine on a 30-day cruise only surfaced four hours.

Because of unusual hull design and double-sized batteries, they could go at far greater speed under water than we could attain — approximately 18 knots — while being relatively slow on the surface (the reverse of ours).

Their living quarters were extremely bad. U.S. cruisers would never have stood for them.

We then drove through the bombed out section of Bremen. The devastation was acute, although the space along the docks (the cranes, etc.) was undamaged. The people, however, looked very well, full of health, and well-fed. They had none of that pinched, hurrying look of the Berliners.

They get no coal, however, and their present diet from us is about 1,200 calories — ours being 4,000. However, they have large reserves which they can draw on.

The fraternization is as frequent as in Berlin. People do not seem to realize how fortunate they have been in escaping the Russians. As far as looting the homes and the towns, however, the British and ourselves have been very guilty.

In spite of the apparent well-being of the people, however, there still remains the question "How well will they do this winter?"

NOTE:

The Congressional Committee under Luther Johnson came through here on a fact-finding tour. According to the Naval personnel, all they were interested in were lugers and cameras.

July 31, 1945

Spent the day in Bremen talking to Navy officials and to the heads of military government in this area.

Among other things, the Navy had accurate reports on German E boats which correspond to our PT boats. The German boat was approximately 105 feet — engines developed 6,000 horse power — had four torpedo tubes and a gun equivalent to our 40 mm — a couple of 20 mm's and some light machine guns.

In speed they ranged from 42 knots to 49 knots in actual trials. Their cruising range was about 700 miles at 35 knots — their displacement about 115 tons — their engines were Diesel.

These figures demonstrate that the German E boat

was far superior to our PT boat. It was 25 feet longer, just as fast, nearly twice as heavy, and had greater cruising range at high speed — in armament it was about equal. Their boat is a better heavy-water boat, cheaper to operate because it burns oil instead of gasoline — and for the same reason, safer from fire or explosion.

The officials in the military government seemed most efficient and sensible in their approach. Evidently, Bremen and Berlin draw the top teams. They were employing Germans as much as possible after first weeding out the party members. They found the Germans extremely willing, almost docile in accepting directions. They had a passion for accuracy, and they had an involved price and wage scale which was thorough and worked well.

In this connection, the Army released several prisoners who had three-year sentences for killing one of their pigs without government permission.

The chief of our government mission felt that the present ration of 1,200 calories was insufficient; it bred hunger and led to black markets (of which at present there were only a few) and dissatisfaction and made their task that much more difficult.

He hoped to get the schools opened by September up to the eighth grade but anticipated difficulty in securing the proper teachers as most of the old ones were strong

Nazis. As far as the percentage of Nazis in the town, it was about 5 per cent.

The city of Bremen was a port city and, therefore, dependent on the surrounding country, much of which was under British control for its food.

The British had been extremely cooperative as far as exchanging food-stuffs. So far little food in this area had been sent to the relief of Berlin, but they were planning to send some dried fish that they had taken from the Germans.

The British had gone into Bremen ahead of us — and everyone was unanimous in their description of British looting and destruction which had been very heavy. They had taken everything which at all related to the sea — ships, small boats, lubricants, machinery, etc.

The military missions finance man was a former director of a small bank in the Mid-West. He was an intelligent man and seemed in every way to be excellent for the job. He said that all financing for the Occupations and for the repair of ships was being paid for by the city of Bremen and the Reichsbanks local branch.

FIGURES:

The amount on hand at time of occupations held by city of Bremen — 72,000,000 R. Marks (securities, etc.)

ınt on hand at time of occupations in Reichs tax
e — 21,000,000 marks

The cost of American occupations to this date (repair
of ships, labor pay) 1,600,000 marks of which Reich
tax office paid 1,000,000 marks

The City of Bremen — 600,000 marks

Income from first three months of fiscal year of
Reich tax office (April, May, and June of 1944)
—   32,000,000 marks

In same period for 1945
—   2,500,000 marks
—8%

* Reichsmarks in value as far as labor pay and price is
equivalent to 2½ Reichsmarks to the dollar.

He found that Germans were good workers, the
bureaucratic administration setup in the town of
Bremen was complicated but efficient with municipal
ownership that was wide-spread.

People had commenced paying taxes and the city was
being run as nearly as possible as before — with the same
wages being paid.

He found that there seemed to be no central plan among our officers. Some treated Germans as a conquered people and got bad results. He believed in treating them as any other employee and found in that way he got the best work. He said that there were as yet few black markets but they should increase during winter. Like everyone else he said that the coal shortage was acute. People were cutting wood to heat their food but in the winter the Germans would be in a desperate situation.

NOTES:

A. Americans looted towns heavily on arrival.

B. American plan seems to be to get things started so that the Germans can look out for themselves; to remove all those with Nazi connections (this in some cases removes the most efficient administrators) and to try to keep Germany divided into separate administrative units.

C. The people looked well here and reasonably cheerful — a great change from Berlin.

D. None of the officers and men here seem to have any particular hate for the Germans, although some throw their weight around.

E. I am quite surprised to see with what zest the German girls, who can be very attractive, throw themselves at the Americans. I cannot believe it would be this way in England or America if the situation were reversed. They argue that there haven't been any men around for four years and it is merely biological.

F. Passing over the German countryside one sees rows and rows of trees, all in orderly groups of different sizes. Trees obviously are considered a crop as much as corn. We could learn a lesson from that in conservation.

G. The docility of the German bureaucrats demonstrates how easy it would be to seize power in Germany. They have not the inquisitive minds of the Americans and the instinctive "I'm from Missouri" attitude towards authority.

August 1, 1945

We flew from Bremen to Frankfurt and were met at the airport by a Battalion of Paratroopers and General Eisenhower. The troops were as well drilled as any I have seen. In fact, all the troops that I have seen in Germany have been outstanding.

We drove to the Farben building which was completely untouched, though surrounded by ruins. Eisenhower talked with Forrestal for a few minutes, and it was obvious why he is an outstanding figure. He has an easy personality, immense self-assurance, and gave an excellent presentation of the situation in Germany.

He said that the situation was complicated by the fact that the Russians in the East have the major food-producing area in Germany while the British, French, and United States in the West were strong on steel, coal, iron, and manufacturing centers but were deficient in food.

The British section was about 40 per cent self-sufficient — we in the South were about 70 per cent self-sufficient. This economic diversification of Germany is what caused Bismarck in 1870 to unite Germany into one unit, which by nature it is. The same factors are facing those people who advocate the breaking up of Germany into old principalities.

In Frankfurt deep underground in the salt mine was found nearly $300,000,000 in gold, silver, securities, and other loot. There was gold from Hungary and France. France is claiming most of it.

There were securities from France and the other countries of the world. We visited it and it was piled brick on brick — bag on bag — in the cellar of the Reichsmark. Its ultimate disposal is still undecided.

NOTE:
So far, there has been no negotiation with the Russians about how much Occupation money will be printed. They have been printing marks wholesale in Berlin, they pay 4,000 marks for a watch which we have been cashing in at the rate of 10 for a dollar.

From Frankfurt we flew to Salzburg, where King Leopold was detained, and drove to the town of Berchtesgaden. It is a beautiful town in the mountains — the houses are alpine in architecture, and the people are well-fed and healthy. There is no bomb damage and there is plenty of wood to take the place of coal. It is a town apart from the destruction of war. We stayed at a beautiful inn for the evening after dining with the local General at the lavishly furnished building that was formerly the headquarters of General Kietal. It was reported that there were six miles of corridors underneath the main building.

The dinner consisted of about six courses — Rhine wines and champagne. After dinner they brought out some cigars taken from Goering's armored car.

In the morning we went up to Hitler's mountain home. It was completely gutted, the result of an air attack from 12,000 pound bombs by the R.A.F. in an attempt on Hitler's life.

Leaving the chalet, we drove to the very top of the mountains (about 7,000 feet) where the famed Eagle's lair was located. The road up was covered with solid rock in many places and was cleverly camouflaged. On arrival at the top, we entered a long tunnel carved through the rocks and came to an elevator which took us up through solid rock for the last 600 feet. The elevator was a double-decker — a space being left on the lower deck for the SS guard.

The lair itself had been stripped of its rugs, pictures, and tapestries, but the view was beautiful — the living room being round and facing out on every side on the valley below.

After visiting these two places, you can easily understand how that within a few years Hitler will emerge from the hatred that surrounds him now as one of the most significant figures who ever lived.

He had boundless ambition for his country which rendered him a menace to the peace of the world, but he had a mystery about him in the way that he lived and in the manner of his death that will live and grow after him. He had in him the stuff of which legends are made.

The Handwritten Pages

Editor's Note: Most of the diary is typed. In addition there are twelve handwritten pages. Only the first, which we have placed at the beginning of the diary section of this volume, concerns Europe. Much of the other eleven pages, of uncertain date, consists of jotted notes not always easy to comprehend. Yet we transcribe them here because there are nuggets of interest. JFK is clearly thinking through the beginning of his political career, which would start with his first run for Congress, in which he was successful, in 1946, just a year after the trip to Europe chronicled in the diary. He makes, or records, wry, and sometimes irritable remarks about other political figures, including Truman ("deader than Kelsey's nuts"), records his opinion of a certain corporate management ("notoriously stupid"), notes the low opinion some local Boston pols have of his ambitions

("Says I'll get murdered") and reflects on the moral character of politicians generally.

The first page transcribed below (the second of all the handwritten pages) is apparently the notes for or from a lecture or presentation JFK was to give or which he heard, amounting to a "School of instruction for politicians."

In this transcription we have striven to give an idea of how the words appeared on the page, while simplifying for readability. Heavy black lines indicate page breaks.

School of instruction for politicians

Date	Feb 7+8 — 10 2:30 8pm

Impress	**I know Christian Social Teaching**
	Appraisal of common picture—
	1–Full Employment
	2–Housing
	3–Wages
	4–Em...[?]—[Talk or Jack Donnelly?]
okay	
afternoon	**Guaranteed annual wages**
	Wages per item
	labor relations

[?] [?]   Social Security
               Pending [?] [?]

afternoon — Problem facing [?] workshops
Evening — Stress ethics + government

Showing that the church is into
National Catholic Welfare
Social [?] Committee

Meeting at New England Mutual Hall
No endorsement — open to public
Regardless of race creed + color

Rev Dan T. McConigle — Professor of
Sociology — [?] + Seminary

---

8 Water St.
St. Vincent de
Paul
James Hurley

EDITOR'S NOTE: There was a family of Tierneys promi-
nent in Boston politics. There is no indication which
member of the family is here referred to.

Jan 23

Conversation with Tierney

Wants me to give money for families
[?] ~~worker~~ striker
strikes are due to Truman's failure
to get G.M. To come through
GM notoriously stupid.
Thinks it will be popular thing
in Time:

Remember Roosevelt's principle that
you have to keep politicians +
policies apart.

Ed Kelly the only really smart pol,
Pols can't tell what is going to happen.
GM strike will last for two more
months.

"Truman is deader than Kelsey's nuts"

AFL is going to follow through
depending on success of CIO

Walter   [?].

Says no — bad politics
First five or six months important
AFL district

Don't push late collective
bargaining to the point of res stage

Jan 27

Conversation with Dan O'Brian
Says I'll get murdered—
No political experience—
A personal district. Says
I don't know 300 people
personally. Says I should
become Mike [?]'s
Secy.

O'Brian indicates the attack
on me will be

1. Inexperience.
2. Injury to role on me in father's reputation.

He is the first man to say bet me
that I can't win!

An honest Irishman but

---

a mistaken one

"In politics you don't
have friends — you have
confederates."

One day they feed you honey —
the next will find
fish caught in your throat.

You can buy brains but
you can't pay — loyalty.

Plant [mulch?]

Lingers McClery — [?]
No I wouldn't stop.

EDITOR'S NOTE: The next several pages seem to consist of a list of books, with catalog numbers, that Kennedy was reading, or intended to read. *Why England Slept,* of course, was written by Kennedy himself.

Ireland + the [Pres?] of the U.S.
John Regan   4518.392.1

Ireland + H.
✔   Patrick William Morris
**   355-9-135**

*Ireland in America — I 184
**   .I 6R7**
[A?] Edward Fergus
Ireland the World Over   *DA 913
**   .W33**

✔ Ireland's Contribution to the law —
✔ Hugh Carney   2418.45

Irish American History of the U.S.
**   John O'Hanlon   2321.115**

Irish Constitution   4414.335

✔ Thomas Maginness

✔ The Irish American

Bryan Bennett

          No 1 in   4511.103

✔ The Irish in America
          Thomas Dowd.   4317.31

✔ Irish in America
          James Farley — no 6 in
                 4226.491

✔ [Moorefred?] H. Rey —
          Americans of Irish Heritage
              4518.288

Irish in U.S. — DA 919.W37
          George Waldren

Why England Slept   DA 578
               .K4

James Walsh

> DA 925.W3

World's [?] the Irish

"The best politician is the
man who does not think too
much of the political consequences
of his every act."

Farley

Democratic party has survived
because –Wilson– "it had a
heart in its jacket"

"The one great failure in American govt
is the govt of critics."

Mr. Bruce — America [?]

Harry Pokat
251 Chamberlain St.
West End

Shipping Companies — a company man —
                     permanent
                     employer
10 years — worked for Ocean Steamship —
Formerly a long-shoreman-union

James F. O'Brien
231 Lexington Ave
Cambridge   Eli 1285

Joseph L. ~~Riord~~ Reardon
30 Aberdeen Ave
Cambridge – Eli 0870

NOTES

THE SAN FRANCISCO CONFERENCE
JULY 10, 1945

This first typewritten page of the diary, dated July 10, 1945, written in England, refers to the United Nations Conference in San Francisco that JFK attended during April and May 1945. This assignment was arranged by his father, Joseph P. Kennedy, through his connections with the Hearst newspapers. JFK was asked to cover the birth of the United Nations "from the point of view of the ordinary GI." Lt. Kennedy had been released from active duty on March 1, 1945, after three and a half years in the Navy. His health problems—particularly his bad back, which had plagued him through the war years, and for which he had recently had a disc operation—forced his early retirement.

The young reporter was not sanguine about the future of the UN or its ability to enforce the peace. In one of the stories he filed from San Francisco, May 7, he wrote:

The world organization that will come out of San Francisco will be the product of the same passion and selfishness that produced the Treaty of Versailles.

There is here, however, one ray of shining bright light. That is the realization, felt by all the delegates, that humanity cannot afford another war.

At the conference Kennedy came in contact with current and future leaders, including Anthony Eden, future prime minister; Chip Bohlen of the State Department; Averell Harriman, U.S. ambassador to Moscow; and Adlai Stevenson, special assistant to the secretary of state.

Few Kennedy biographers have given much attention to this period from April to August 1945, or taken much note of JFK's brief journalistic career. Yet as Theodore Sorensen in his biography, *Kennedy*, writes succinctly:

In a brief fling at journalism he had observed power politics at Potsdam and the San Francisco UN Conference and covered the British elections. All this sharpened his interest in public affairs and public service.

Two of Kennedy's close White House political aides, Kenneth P. O'Donnell and David F. Powers, in their book *Johnny, We Hardly Knew Ye,* credit these few months as a journalist for much that would happen later:

The thing that finally moved Jack Kennedy toward active politics, as he said later, was not trying to carry on for Joe or "my father's eyes on the back of my neck," but his own experience as a correspondent at the United Nations Conference in San Francisco and at Potsdam, which sharpened his interest in the national and international issues of the coming postwar period. After getting a close look as a reporter at the postwar political leaders in action, he decided that he might be able to find more satisfaction and to perform more useful service as a politician than as a political writer or a teacher of government and history, the two careers that he had been considering up to that time.

JFK's argument here against those who would go to war with Russia immediately is not strategic but political: Democracy cannot effectively wage war until the citizens are persuaded there is no alternative.

The related notion that Chamberlain deserved much credit for bringing the U.S. into the war and that he paved the way for Churchill is certainly unusual. Most observers at the time and since regarded Chamberlain as weak and vacillating, and his appeasement policy that culminated in the abandonment of Czechoslovakia—"Peace in Our Time"—a disaster. The conventional wisdom holds that had Chamberlain not met each of Hitler's overtures and instead stood by Czechoslovakia and built up Britain's defenses, war could have been averted.

JFK's unusually positive assessment of Chamberlain in 1945 was probably influenced by his father's close liaison with Chamberlain and his inner circle in 1939 and 1940, while ambassador to the Court of St. James.

Only six years earlier JFK had been, in effect, under his father's tutelage. Father and son had attended the debate in Parliament in August 1939 when Chamberlain tried to explain his failed policy of appeasement with Hitler. When JFK returned to Harvard in the fall he wrote a pro-Chamberlain editorial for the *Crimson* entitled "Peace in Our Time," about which Nigel Hamilton, author of *Reckless Youth*, comments: "Jack's intentions were sincere. He had hoped Roosevelt would, through his father in London, attempt to secure peace at any price rather than a war in which Britain and France might be destroyed. However, Jack's editorial reflected also his father's defeatism."

Eighteen years after he wrote this diary, President Kennedy on April 9, 1963, announced that the United States Congress had granted Sir Winston Churchill honorary citizenship. In an understated yet eloquent message, the president shows the growth of his respect for the leader he had followed all his life. He says: "I only propose a formal recognition of the place he has long since won in the history of freedom and in the affections of my—and now his—fellow countrymen."

JFK was, of course, correct that "the clash with Russia" would "be greatly postponed." It is very unlikely that he could have known about the atomic bomb on this date. President Truman learned about its existence only on April 13, 1945, and gave the top-secret order to drop the bomb on July 24. However, we know that JFK, through his contacts, had been privy to some of the high-level debate over the Russian threat to Europe and Asia and that he understood firepower and sophistication of weaponry as the key to both winning and preventing wars. I saw firsthand the great lengths to which Kennedy went in order to seek out the best minds and most cogent ideas, especially on national security. Scores of papers attest to the thoroughness of his advisors; some of these papers are in the Kennedy Library—still classified. Somehow this constant thirst for information and his own powerful intuition had given him a glimpse of the horrible potentialities that were to dominate his own presidency.

THE BRITISH ELECTION
JUNE 21, 1945

Kennedy was right about the election. The voting took place on July 6; the results, a Labor landslide, were not reported until July 26. In a news story filed on June 23, 1945, JFK predicted: "England is moving towards some form of socialism—if not in this election, then surely at the next. What will be the significance for America if Churchill is defeated by the Labor Party?" Arthur Krock, in his book *Memories,* credits his friend Jack as being the only one to keep him informed of a possible defeat for Churchill. It will, no doubt, be a revelation to some readers that the young reporter was critical of President Roosevelt's economic liberalism. Yet Kennedy, who as both legislator and president showed restraint on social issues such as civil rights, was reluctant to take part in popular causes and was fiscally conservative.

JUNE 29, 1945

Herbert Parmet, in *Jack: The Struggles of John F. Kennedy,* provides crucial insights:

> Kennedy's record did not make him a progressive New Deal Democrat. When dealing in theory, when lecturing about the nature of government, he fell back to the classical liberal doctrines held by his father that had come to seem conservative in the years since they were first formulated. Along with his Whiggish belief in the rule of the elite, he had the liberal's concern for the maximization of freedom for the individual.

Kathleen Kennedy, JFK's sister, had spent the better part of her time in England since 1938. She was married to Lord Hartington, the son of the duke and duchess of Devonshire, in May of 1944; he was killed in battle in August of 1944. Kathleen was a free spirit, adored by her father and older brothers and beloved by the British. Her mother did not sanction her marriage to a Protestant and could never come to terms with her death in an airplane crash in 1949 while on a flight to Paris with her true love, a married man, Lord Fitzwilliam.

It may come as a surprise to many American readers that JFK was a true Anglophile. He spent a good deal of time in England as a young man and had many British friends and a myriad of contacts with important leaders in Britain and elsewhere. JFK studied in England in 1935. He and his friend Lem Billings traveled throughout Europe in 1937, and he spent the summer of 1938 in England. In 1939 he was allowed a six-month leave of absence from his studies at Harvard and spent his time well, working for his father in the embassy office and for Ambassador Bullitt in Paris for a month, and traveling extensively. During 1939 the twenty-two-year-old JFK visited many countries, including Russia, Turkey, Poland, Austria, Hungary, Spain, the Middle East, Czechoslovakia, and Germany. These experiences and the friendships made in those years were a permanent asset. In August of 1959 I was asked to telephone David Ormsby-Gore, British delegate to the United Nations, for Senator Kennedy, to seek Ormsby-Gore's opinion on the ending of nuclear weapons testing. Mr. Ormsby-Gore gave me the information I needed in a polite and crisp manner and then added he would be in touch with Senator Kennedy with further detail. They had met in the 1930s and were close friends.

Lady Violet is Lady Bonham-Carter, daughter of Herbert Asquith, in whose cabinet Winston Churchill served. She was a close personal friend and confidant of Winston Churchill, and an active and dynamic leader in British politics. Her book *Winston Churchill* is a classic picture of Churchill's early years.

Duff-Cooper, in 1938, was first lord of the Admiralty until he resigned in protest of Chamberlain's settlement with Hitler at Munich. Later, William Manchester recorded in *The Last Lion*: "Churchill exulted that 'one minister alone stood forth... At the moment of Mr. Chamberlain's overwhelming mastery of public opinion he thrust his way through the exulting throng to declare his total disagreement with its leader.'"

Duff-Cooper resigned in October of 1938. JFK had returned to his studies at Harvard in September, where he was grappling with the issues of appeasement and intervention in the war. He was also working overtime so that he would be allowed to take a half-year off to spend in England and the continent—which he did—returning on February 9, 1939.

JFK's summary of the duke of Devonshire's views on India reminds us that in his earlier travels JFK met the future viceroy and governor general of India, Lord Louis Mountbatten, who would preside over India's departure from the Empire. At the time of this diary Mountbatten was one of the three Supreme Allied Commanders (along with Eisenhower and MacArthur). He was a participant at the Potsdam Conference.

In *Mountbatten,* his biography of the former viceroy, Philip Ziegler recounts Lord Mountbatten's visit with President

Kennedy in the Oval Office in 1961 when the president reminded his Navy soul mate that they had met in London before the war:

> The following year, however, Eisenhower gave way to Kennedy. Mountbatten did not meet him till April 1961 when Kennedy asked him whether he remembered that as a young student before the war he had been a guest at the Brook House penthouse. "For the sake of Anglo-U.S. amity I lied and said 'yes'," wrote Mountbatten. The visit, supposed to be a courtesy call taking five minutes, instead lasted fifty. "I formed the highest possible impression of Mr. Kennedy, who seemed to be realistic and sound on everything we discussed," recorded Mountbatten in his diary.

JUNE 30, 1945

In the first paragraph JFK substituted the word "hearts" for "life" in his handwriting.

Though some biographers have written of enmity between Eisenhower and Kennedy, the comments in the diary suggest the respect the younger man had for the older. Sorensen notes that President Kennedy asked the former president to meet with him during or soon after crises such as the Bay of Pigs, the Cuban missile crisis or the civil rights crucible. Hugh Sidey, in his book *John F. Kennedy, President,* written in 1963, paints a picture of at least a respectful relationship between the two leaders. Sidey, who as a reporter had covered JFK for six years, tells of President Eisenhower at the transition meeting in the Cabinet room at the White House glancing at the map of Southeast Asia and saying, "This is one of the problems I'm leaving you that I'm not happy about. We may have to fight." Sidey also notes that both men recognized the potential threat of a Russian war machine left unchallenged:

Coffee with Dwight and Mamie Eisenhower, then at last the two most important citizens of the United States began the famous mile from the White House to the Capitol. From someplace beside the White House the strains of "America" drifted out over the snow. As he rode to the Capitol, Kennedy listened to Eisenhower at his side. The retiring president told him that somehow he had felt the Russians never would start a war if this country remained firm enough.

In this entry "reporter" John F. Kennedy mentions Churchill's book *The World Crisis*. According to Herbert Parmet, Kay Halle, who visited young Kennedy in the Massachusetts General Hospital when he was fifteen, found him surrounded by books piled high and reading *The World Crisis*. He later told her he had read everything Churchill wrote.

British biographer Nigel Hamilton, writing of Churchill and Kennedy in *JFK: Reckless Youth*, says:

There were other similarities between young Kennedy and Churchill, not the least of which was Jack's reportorial quest, which demonstrated something of the same animation that had driven the young Winston Churchill in earlier years as a newspaper correspondent, after his combat experience on the North–West Frontier, in the Sudan, and in the Boer War, before he stood for Parliament.

Witnessing Churchill's uphill struggle in the summer of 1945, at the very apogee of his political career, however, taught Jack an important lesson. What had been almost unimaginable while in America—that Churchill and his Conservative government should fall at the general election—had become all too understandable once he witnessed war-torn, bankrupt Britain and, at last, the plight of ordinary people.

Kennedy as candidate and as President often quoted Churchill and even practiced some of his rhetoric to reflect the Churchillian style. In his speech "The Years the Locusts Have Eaten," given in Milwaukee, Wisconsin, on November 13, 1959, Senator Kennedy began his address with the words:

Twenty-three years ago in a bitter debate in the House of
Commons, Winston Churchill charged the British Government with
acute blindness to the menace of Nazi Germany, with gross negli-
gence in the maintenance of the island's defenses, and with indifferent, indecisive leadership of British foreign policy and British
public opinion. The preceding years of drift and impotency, he said,
were "the years the locusts have eaten."

JULY 1, 1945

William Douglas-Home was the brother of Alec Douglas-
Home, a future prime minister. Lord Beaverbrook, a famous
financier and politician, owned the *Daily Express.*

JFK had met William Douglas-Home through his sister
Kathleen; he was one of her many English admirers. The significance of this entry is the thought that JFK picked up from
Douglas-Home on the growing threat of the Russian pres-
ence in Europe. He paraphrases Douglas-Home as saying "we
made it possible for Russia to obtain that very dominance
that we fought Germany to prevent her having."

JULY 2, 1945

JFK's comments on the "movements to the Left" and the
"radicals of the Left" whom he associates with "[the] spirit
which builds dictatorships" prompts consideration of who
shaped JFK's thinking.

The education Jack Kennedy received at Harvard was crucial to his intellectual development. His professors knew him
well, enjoyed his independence of mind, and gave him
detailed advice on his courses.

One of those at Harvard who had a profound influence on

Jack Kennedy was his tutor, Professor Bruce Hopper. Hopper was the author of the book *Pan-Sovietism*, published in 1931. The book is based on the Lowell Lectures given by Professor Hopper on the background of Bolshevism and his informed speculation on the future relations of Russia with the United States and the Orient. Hopper's study is in large part based on his extensive travels through Russia and his intense interest in the Russian people and their oppressive governmental system.

In his book Professor Hopper predicts:

> It may well be that the decisive battle between capitalism and social-ism, between individualism and collectivism, if it comes to that, will be fought out, not in Europe or America, but in the fluid East, where economic systems are still in the making. According to pre-sent indications the probable economic antagonists will be America and Soviet Russia.

In a summary note to his readers, clearly well grasped by his young student Kennedy, Professor Hopper writes:

> We can avoid certain major pitfalls in the situation if we distinguish between the problems inherent in land and people, and the prob-lems superimposed by the Communists.

Nigel Hamilton, in his book *Reckless Youth*, credits Bruce Hopper's guidance for Jack's close analysis of "Russian com-munism as well as German and Italian fascism." He writes:

> Though he would be an avid reader all his life, Jack's intensive courses in twentieth-century isms—capitalism, communism, fascism, imperialism, militarism, nationalism—were probably the most con-centrated academic study he would ever undertake.

JULY 3, 1945

Harold Laski was a political science professor at the London
School of Economics (1926–50). JFK, in London with his
father and sister Kathleen in the summer of 1935, enrolled in
a course with Professor Laski, but found it boring and
returned to the United States in October. Laski's political
views were considered Marxist and too far left for many in
the Labor Party which he served.

JULY 24, 1945

The visit to Ireland was arranged by Ambassador Kennedy
through the State Department. He was very anxious that the
trip come off well since plans were already in the making for
JFK's run for Congress and an Irish trip would be invaluable
politically.

It appears that JFK spent most of June and July in England
and that during part of that time he was not well. He left for
Ireland on July 23.

Ambassador Kennedy was a close friend of the prime minister of Ireland, Eamon de Valera. The prime minister had
been a special guest of the Kennedy family at the coronation
of Pope Pius XII in 1938. JFK met de Valera at that gathering.

This was his first visit to Ireland, but JFK was by no means
a novice in the history and politics of his ancestral home. In
February 1941, for example, he wrote an article for the *New
York Journal American* explaining the roots of Irish refusal to
cooperate with England during the war:

> Winston Churchill [who] was Minister for War, dispatched the Black
> and Tans who scourged Ireland for three years. Ireland has not for-
> gotten this, and remembers further that in 1938 Mr. Churchill also led

the group who opposed the return of the ports to Ireland. They do not
feel they can depend on him to restore them once the war is over.

The Dail is the Irish parliament.

Ireland, as JFK mentions in the diary, remained neutral
during World War II. Belfast suffered some heavy bombing
by the Germans in 1941, with loss of lives and buildings.
Nevertheless Prime Minister de Valera did not wish the
United States to enter the war against Germany and encouraged American isolationists.

Ambassador David Gray, with whom JFK stayed on this
1945 trip to Dublin (he calls him "Minister" not
"Ambassador"), was a close personal friend of President
Roosevelt, a strong supporter of Great Britain, and skeptical
of de Valera. He urged President Roosevelt to seize the naval
bases in Ireland. De Valera refused to deliver the bases.

Young reporter Kennedy interviewed both Ambassador
Gray and Prime Minister de Valera. When on page 15 of the
diary he says "Churchill's speech at the end of the war, in
which he attacked de Valera, was extraordinarily indiscreet,"
JFK is referring to Prime Minister Churchill's broadcast of
May 13, 1945:

> This was indeed a deadly moment in our life, and if it had not been
> for the loyalty and friendship of Northern Ireland, we should have
> been forced to come to close quarters with Mr. de Valera, or perish
> forever from the earth. However, with a restraint and poise to
> which, I say, history will find few parallels, His Majesty's
> Government never laid a hand on them, though at times it would
> have been quite easy, and quite natural.

Because of his father's position as ambassador to Great
Britain, JFK had had a front-row seat to the events leading up

to war's outbreak. When Ambassador Kennedy first arrived in England in early 1938, he was enthusiastically received. He was the perfect man for the job—an outgoing bon vivant who could charm the English. And in the beginning, with his attractive family in tow, he did just that. However, as time went on and the threat of a Nazi takeover of Europe became more pressing, Ambassador Kennedy sank into his preconceived belief that for the U.S. and England economic survival required appeasement. This led to the ambassador's well-known political liaison with Prime Minister Chamberlain and his somewhat questionable public and private negotiations outside of diplomatic channels.

At the time, the twenty-two-year-old JFK was both working for his father and traveling extensively. In Berlin in late August 1939, JFK and his friend Torbert Macdonald were almost arrested by German stormtroopers. Instead JFK ended up carrying back to his father the official diplomatic message from the chargé d'affaires, Alex Kirk, that war would break out within a week.

IMPRESSION OF BRITISH ELECTION RESULTS
JULY 27, 1945

The British election of 1945, called by Churchill only three months after the Nazis surrendered, was a watershed. This diary entry records JFK's analysis of the election accompanied by statistics. There was probably no young American reporter better suited to cover this historic confrontation between conservatives and liberals in Britain. He had studied British history, had lived in England during a good part of his

mature life, and wrote his college thesis on the British political struggle prior to World War II. While covering the birth
of the United Nations in San Francisco, JFK got to know the
British delegation and interviewed them on the upcoming
election. In his story for the Hearst newspapers, headlined
"British Election Held Vital to U.S.," filed on May 28, 1945,
JFK reported:

> It is difficult to judge the result at present. The British delegation
> here is pretty well split in its opinions. It is Britain's first general
> election since the Conservatives won in 1935. There are millions of
> young voters who will be voting for the first time and no one is sure
> which way they'll go. In addition while Churchill's strength is undis-
> puted, it is not certain he can buck the recent surge to the left.

While in England in the summer of 1945, JFK interviewed
scores of well-informed British leaders, sampled public opinion, listened to Churchill's stump speeches, and attended
intimate political gatherings. There was less interest in the
British elections in the U.S. than had been anticipated by the
Hearst newspapers—some of the stories filed by JFK went
unused. JFK notes that if the radical left—i.e., "Laski, Shinwell
and Cripps"—dominated the Labor Party, it would fail.
Shinwell was minister of defense under Prime Minister Atlee.
Sir Stafford Cripps was a leftist in the Labor Party and was
chancellor of the exchequer from 1947–50.

NOTES ON FRANCE
JULY 28, 1945

France in July of 1945 was recovering from her humiliation in
World War II. After the French government failed to effec-

tively mobilize the mighty French army and the much-touted Maginot Line proved impotent, the government signed an armistice with Hitler in June of 1940. Marshall Petain became the new French premier. The French underground fought bravely throughout the war and gave vital assistance to the Allies; Charles de Gaulle was given refuge in Britain.

JFK's comment that the French people were disappointed in de Gaulle reflects the view of the French leader abroad. The British were fed up with de Gaulle's ego during the war; Churchill referred to him as his "Cross of Lorraine." President Truman, however, recognized the strategic role of France in the postwar recovery. With British cooperation the United States made certain that Stalin's desire to neutralize France was quashed by allowing the French a role in the United Nations and in the reconstruction of Germany.

JFK's theme of a threat from the French left is backed up by the contemporary observations of Forrestal, with whom he was traveling. In the *Forrestal Diaries* we learn that:

> Forrestal dined in Paris on the evening of July 27 with Jefferson Caffery, the American Ambassador to France, and others. From Caffery he heard that "the only people in France with a positive line of attack are the Communists under Thorez and Duclos." He said the Russian Ambassador, Bogomolov, is "quite candid in admitting the direction of the French Communists by Moscow." Caffery said he had told the President that unless France got some coal from the United States for the coming winter "there would inevitably be Communism and possibly anarchy."

Likewise, JFK's gloomy assessment of the financial situation is reflected in Forrestal's reporting on the meeting with Dean Jay at Morgans' on page 77 of his diary:

Next morning Forrestal "saw Dean Jay at Morgan's," who told him "there was no leadership left among the top industrial people in France; they were all under constant attack and all very discouraged.... There is a great inertia still over the people. They are not taking hold with either vigor or firmness."

Forrestal, a former Wall Street friend of Ambassador Joseph Kennedy, was meeting with the top financial expert in Paris, Dean Jay at Morgan's. The Morgan bank had snubbed Kennedy at every juncture as an "Irish Papist and a Wall Street punter." Even after Ambassador Kennedy initiated the 1939 prewar visit of the king and queen of England to America, Jack Morgan made certain that his nemesis did not receive an invitation to the historic royal visit.

Now, six years later in this little-known visit to Paris, the ambassador's son was sharing views with those in the financial world who would play a formidable role in reshaping postwar Europe.

Interestingly, Ron Chenow, in his highly acclaimed book, *The House of Morgan*, writes:

Morgan et Compagnie was the sole American bank in Paris to stay open throughout the war. It even turned a small profit. Leonard Rist was smart enough to see that such success might smack of collaboration, or at least of moral corner cutting. Perhaps as a result, he frequently cited his decoration from General Eisenhower for "gallant service in assisting the escape of Allied soldiers from the enemy." That the U.S. Government approved Morgan et Compagnie's wartime conduct was confirmed in late 1944 when the Treasury and War departments asked J.P. Morgan and Company to send senior Paris partner Dean Jay and other Americans back to the Place Vendome to restore a semblance of normality. Of the small, white-haired Dean Jay, it was said that American businessmen in France seldom made a major move without consulting him, and so his return carried symbolic weight. In the highest tribute of all, Morgan et Compagnie was assigned to handle deposits for American troops in liberated France.

GERMANY
JULY 29, 1945

The Potsdam meeting of the big three powers—the United States, Britain, and the USSR—was held in Germany in July 1945. The purpose was to decide the major issues facing post-war Europe and Russia's entry into the war against Japan. Instead, it turned out to be, in effect, the start of the cold war.

It was at Potsdam that the new president met Churchill and Stalin for the first time. It was also at this meeting that President Truman told Stalin the United States had an atomic bomb, and it was here in his "Little White House" in Babelsberg that the president made his final decision to drop the bomb on Japan.

Many seasoned diplomats tried to warn President Truman of the dangers he faced from Stalin at Potsdam. Churchill had sent him the famous cable in May warning of "The Iron Curtain between us and everything to the eastward." Averell Harriman, U.S. ambassador to Moscow, briefed the president on the global threat of communism.

It was into this charged atmosphere that Secretary of the Navy Forrestal, an uninvited guest, flew into Gatow Airport on July 28 with his friend, John F. Kennedy. The trip with the Navy Secretary had been finalized by Ambassador Joseph Kennedy while his son was still in Ireland.

Forrestal was deeply concerned about the Russians' post-war machinations, both military and political, and he intended to tell the President what he thought. He had discussed Russian intentions and the results of the British elections with JFK, and they were to tour parts of war-torn Germany in the next few days.

Kennedy says that the same honor guard that the new prime minister inspected was inspected by the prime minister a "few days before." That would have been Churchill, who had just been defeated in his election and had returned from Potsdam to London. JFK mentions stopping in front of the president's house. Margaret Truman, in her book *Harry S. Truman,* mentions the "Little White House" in Babelsberg as the place where her father made the final decision to drop the atomic bomb:

> Landing at Antwerp on July 15, Dad and his party flew to Gatow Airfield, ten miles from the Berlin suburb of Babelsberg, where he was to stay. The conference had long been called the "Berlin meeting," but too much of the German capital had been destroyed to permit any sizable gathering there. So the Russians selected Potsdam, about twenty-five miles from Berlin, as a less damaged site, and chose a number of palatial houses in nearby Babelsberg for residences. By nightfall Dad was settled into a three-story yellow stucco house, which formerly belonged to the head of the German movie industry. It was on a lake swarming with mosquitoes. Prime Minister Churchill had another large house only a few blocks away, and Stalin was also nearby.

It is a remarkable footnote to history that JFK probably had more "inside" information on crucial world events in July of 1945 than did the new president who was preparing for the Potsdam Conference. The young reporter had spent the prewar years either working for his father at the embassy in London or traveling, sometimes on particular diplomatic chores, and had attended the San Francisco Conference as a reporter, covered Churchill's 1945 re-election campaign, and was now in Germany as a guest of Navy Secretary Forrestal.

When President Truman took over the most powerful office in the world on April 12, 1945, after President Roosevelt's sudden death, he had not been briefed on major issues. He knew nothing about the concessions Roosevelt had made to Stalin at the Tehran and Yalta conferences, and he was unaware of the seriousness of the Russian threat. As David McCullough, in *Truman*, summarizes the situation:

> Truman had had no experience in relations with Britain or Russia, no firsthand knowledge of Churchill or Stalin. He didn't know the right people. He didn't know Harriman. He didn't know his own Secretary of State, more than to say hello. He had no background in foreign policy, no expert or experienced advisers of his own to call upon for help. Most obviously, he was not Franklin Roosevelt. How many times would that be said, thought, written?
>
> Roosevelt had done nothing to keep him informed or provide background on decisions and plans at the highest levels. Roosevelt, Truman would tell Margaret privately, "never did talk to me confidentially about the war, or about foreign affairs or what he had in mind for peace after the war." He was unprepared, bewildered. And frightened.

The young reporter, Kennedy, had the unique opportunity of meeting many of the key leaders on the international stage—Churchill, Eisenhower, Truman, Atlee, Bevin, de Valera, and Gromyko. He had discussed the pressing foreign policy issues of the day with Averell Harriman, Herbert Morrison, Hugh Fraser, Harold Laski, and Chip Bohlen. Whereas, McCullough points out:

> Truman had never met Harriman. Until now, nor had he ever really worked with anyone of such background. Harriman was another new experience, and the first of several men of comparable education and eastern polish—Charles Bohlen, John J. McCloy, James Forrestal, Dean Acheson, Robert A. Lovett—who were to play vital roles in Truman's administration. Even the redoubtable Henry Stimson was as yet to Truman a remote presence.

In the summer of 1945 the city of Berlin was in shambles. Approximately one-half of the population of more than four million had been killed in the war. Many of those remaining, mostly elderly and children, were malnourished and beleaguered. The recovery that was just beginning was delayed by the Russian occupation.

The decision to allow the Russian Army to enter Berlin first was made by President Roosevelt in April of 1945, despite protests from Churchill. General Eisenhower, supreme commander of the Allied forces in Europe, was obliged to order Generals Patton and Montgomery to hold back. As a result of their political victory, the Soviets gained a valuable foothold in Berlin. They plundered the city and committed atrocities against the civilian population.

This entry reflects the volatile situation unfolding in Berlin in the summer of 1945. The division of Germany into four zones and the creation of a military government had been decided upon at Yalta. The Russians were to control East Germany; the United States, Britain, and France were to divide up the West. The city of Berlin, deep inside the Russian zone, was planned for joint control by all four powers.

JFK predicts that the Russians are going to make their part of Germany a Soviet Socialist Republic. He muses over the dilemma posed by, on the one hand, leaving the Germans alone to accomplish their own economic revival and the danger, on the other hand, "if we pull out and leave a political vacuum that the Russians will be only too glad to fill."

These were prophetic words. World War II was over in

Europe but there was a new conflict emerging that would dominate Western policy for the next fifty years. During the Berlin crisis in June of 1961, when President Kennedy laid down his ultimatum to Khrushchev, he was greeted by the Russian leader's angry outburst:

> Tell Kennedy if he starts a war he will probably become the last President of the United States.

IMPRESSION OF BERLIN RUINS

Unter den Linden is a famous thoroughfare in Berlin, similar to Fifth Avenue in New York City, with large shops and tall buildings. It has been rebuilt.

JFK's companions on the walk through the ruins of Berlin included Secretary Forrestal, Averell Harriman, and Chip Bohlen. We know from Forrestal's diaries that he and Harriman, at least, had lunch that day at General Lucius D. Clay's visitors' house (Clay was the American military governor in Germany), which Forrestal's group was using as a temporary headquarters. Kennedy may have been at the lunch. Forrestal was along for the trip to Hitler's Reich Chancellery.

The date of the walk through Berlin and the Clay luncheon was Sunday, July 29. The editor of the *Forrestal Diaries* writes:

> On the Monday Forrestal breakfasted with the President—together with Eisenhower, Clay, Judge Samuel Rosenman, *his own naval aides and others*—and what he recorded of the talk was, interestingly enough in view of that meeting with the American armor, mainly about postwar military plans and policies. (emphasis added)

In his recently published book, *The Last Great Victory, The End of World War II, July/August 1945*, Stanley Weintraub concludes:

> Forrestal's breakfast for Truman on the thirtieth brought the Secretary of the Navy's young traveling companion to Potsdam, but John Kennedy did not have the clout to sit at the table with Truman, Eisenhower, and senior American powers then in Germany. It did mean, however, that the two succeeding presidents were in Potsdam with the current one—Eisenhower, who would succeed Truman, and more improbably at the time, Kennedy, who would succeed Eisenhower.

We also know from the Arthur Krock papers at the Seeley Mudd Manuscript Library, Princeton (Hamilton, page 721), that Eisenhower "asked Truman at Potsdam not to beg Russians to come into the war."

Thus in Potsdam we have a sitting president making crucial decisions, including the use of the most powerful weapon yet known to man; the general who would succeed him as president giving him advice; and a young reporter, who would be president in sixteen years, observing both. Remarkably, one of President Kennedy's most acclaimed accomplishments was his successful negotiation of the test-ban treaty with the Russians in 1963.

TALK WITH COL. HOWLIE [HOWLEY], CHIEF OF AMERICAN MILITARY GOVERNMENT IN BERLIN

Captain Frank Howley was chief of the American military government in Berlin from 1945 to 1949. He was General Lucius Clay's top man, charged with thwarting Russian encroachment. In 1947 he was promoted to the rank of brigadier general. In his book *Berlin Command*, Howley tells of the skirmishes over territory in the city, the battles over food distribution, and, finally, the Berlin blockade in 1947.

The interview with Colonel Howley shows the tensions among the occupation forces of the four powers—Britain, France, Russia, and the United States. JFK mentions looting again. This interview strikes a chord similar to Secretary Forrestal's comments on the same tour. In his diary for July 29, 1945, he says:

> went back to Averell's house where I met Ed Pauley, American Ambassador for Reparations, and Chip Bohlen. All hands disturbed by Russian negotiations on reparations. They are stripping every area they are in of all movable goods, and at the same time asking reparations and designating the goods they take as war booty. They are shooting and pressing Germans out of the American district. They shot two... near our house the other night, one woman for refusing to give up her jewelry and attempting to run away. Averell said this... reflected the Russians' indifference to life.

JFK notes Howley's belief that "the American Group" was prevented by the Russians from reaching their zone because the Russians "wanted to continue their looting." Howley reports this same incident in his book; his fifty-man reconnaissance team entering Berlin was stopped by the Russians on the bridge at the Elbe and forced to reduce their numbers.

General Howley resigned from his post in August of 1949. His successor was General Maxwell Taylor, who later became chairman of the Joint Chiefs of Staff in the Kennedy Administration. Howley was, like his friend General George Patton, adamant in his belief that we should not allow ourselves to be pushed around by the Russians. He handled his adversary, Soviet General A. G. Kotikov, with aplomb, as he notes in the last few pages of his book:

When I left Berlin in September, things were normal again. The Russians were behaving exactly as Russians always behave. The Soviet radio was popping its tubes with glee over my resignation as commandant. For some reason, I was suddenly "Howley, the Rough Rider from Texas," and the Russian radio, to the accompaniment of cowboy music, was deriding me for refusing to be drawn into the web again in the Kommandatura...

I rather think that Kotikov will remember our farewell. The Kommandatura had just concluded its meeting and, as the departing chairman, I was host at the inevitable buffet in the next room.

Kotikov had used up a good portion of the meeting complaining about various things, including my "rudeness," but now he was unusually affable. A waiter brought a tray of drinks as we stood talking. Kotikov communed with his ulcers and announced that he wanted a "weak" drink.

"Champagne?" someone asked.

Kotikov puffed out his cheeks and shook his head. "Makes me belch," he said.

"Have a Martini," I said shrewdly.

"What is a Martini?" Kotikov asked.

I pointed to the lethal drink on the tray. Innocently, Kotikov picked it up. I took champagne. Kotikov raised his glass.

"To a successful journey to the United States," he proposed, fairly bursting with glee at the prospect of my leaving. We all drank. To my astonishment, Kotikov gulped the entire contents of his glass—Martini, olive, and all. A look of wonder crossed his face. I proposed a toast. Another Martini clanked down to the Russian's ulcers. There were two more toasts and two more rapid Martinis for Kotikov.

I look at him curiously. His disarmingly cherubic face was twisted. Obviously his stomach was on fire.

I nodded toward another Martini.

"Nyet!" he gasped.

Happily, I steered the suffering Kotikov over to the table. I ran my hand through the gray hair he had given me. At last, we were even.

TALK WITH PIERRE HUSS, CHIEF OF THE INS BUREAU OF BERLIN

In his talk with Pierre Huss, chief of the INS (International News Service) in Berlin, JFK is reflecting the early signs of the Russians' intention to control eastern Europe and use the allied victory over the Nazis to build a stronghold in Berlin and all of East Germany. The situation on the ground in Berlin at this time was chaotic. The heavy bombing raids had knocked out the entire infrastructure of the city. There was no transportation, sanitation, housing, or communications. The civilian population was starving, living in rubble, and plagued with disease. The Russian leadership's retaliation against Nazism gave their soldiers license for looting, raping, and cruelty toward the entire German population. Beyond the disarray in terms of human misery and oppression, we see here the political battle lines being drawn. JFK, in speaking of the communist inroads, says they are "putting it over on us" and "We seem to have no definite policy."

CONVERSATION WITH A GERMAN GIRL

In his interview with a German girl, we find JFK typically inquisitive. He appears to have wrung everything out of her, including her religion, her reading of the situation in Berlin during wartime, and her predictions for the future. One has to wonder if this lady is still alive and if she would remember being interviewed by a future president of the United States.

In August 1939 when JFK was in Berlin staying at the Excelsior Hotel, the Nazis were gearing up for war and he sensed the danger. Now at the time of this diary in July of 1945, as he views the damage, he says "it will be many years before Berlin can clear the wreckage and get the material to rebuild." This, of course, was before President Truman's Marshall Plan, which poured millions of dollars into Germany and all of war-torn Europe.

JFK's worry over a divided Germany, however, was prophetic; it was sixteen years later in July of 1961, on a hot summer day, that he delivered his famous speech to the nation on Berlin and let Premier Khrushchev know that he would not abandon that city or be intimidated by the Russians. In answer to the Soviet military buildup in Berlin he said in part: "I hear it said that West Berlin is militarily untenable. And so was Bastogne. And so, in fact, was Stalingrad. Any dangerous spot is tenable if men—brave men—will make it so." He then called for a heavy increase in military preparedness to which the Congress responded fully. Then in June 1963 the president visited the Berlin wall and in his dramatic and famous speech, he said: "Today, in the world of freedom, the proudest boast is 'Ich bin ein Berliner.' There are some who say that communism is the wave of the future. Let them come to Berlin. And there are some who say in Europe and elsewhere we can work with the Communists. Let them come to Berlin."

BREMEN
JULY 29, 1945

Comparing the dates in the *Forrestal Diaries* with JFK's diary, it appears that the date on this page should have been July 30. To quote from the editor of the *Forrestal Diaries*:

After his talk with Byrnes (July 30), Forrestal left from Gatow airport
in mid-morning for a quick survey of Germany. In the Bremen area
he saw the plants that had been developed for the mass production
of schnorkel-type submarines—there were sixteen of these formidable craft on the ways at the Deschimage yard.

JFK mentions the *Marblehead,* whose former commander
met them at the airport. The USS *Marblehead* was a four-fun-
nelled cruiser. She was badly damaged in the battle of the
Java Sea in February 1942 and had to be returned to the
United States for repairs. The battle of the Java Sea, to defend
the East Indies from the Japanese, took a heavy toll on the
American, Dutch, British, and Australian naval forces.

In speaking of the captured German ship *Europa,* JFK
mentions the raid on Narvik by the British. Narvik, in northern Norway, is beyond the arctic circle. Narvik was one of the
early battles of World War II undertaken in 1940 while
Churchill was first lord of the Admiralty. Norway was neutral,
but Churchill tried to persuade his government to take the
initiative to protect Norwegian territorial waters against the
Germans. The battle of Narvik proved to be a costly and
embarrassing one for the British, but it also cut the German
destroyer fleet in half.

Throughout World War II Germany had submarine technology and production superior to that of the United States.
German boats were superior in overall design, speed, maneu-
verability, and underwater durability. Moreover, the U.S. had
been forced to deploy the largest portion of its submarine
fleet to the Pacific theater, resulting in severe losses to U.S.
supply ships in the Atlantic between 1941 and 1945. In the

arctic campaign the British and American fleets were no match for the German torpedo capability. Both nations suffered enormous casualties bringing supplies and ammunition to the Russian front.

The Germans were the first to initiate the wolfpack, i.e., subs moving in groups, and they perfected submarine pens. Pens were safe underwater refuge cages built along the sides of major harbors and waterways that were resistant to torpedo attacks.

JFK had learned about the dangers of torpedo warfare earlier in his career. In early September of 1939 his father sent him on his first official diplomatic mission, which turned out to be a difficult one. He had to handle outraged Americans who had survived the sinking by a German U-boat of the SS *Athenia* and were demanding convoy escort back to the United States. As the U.S. was still a neutral nation, no convoy was provided. Samuel Eliot Morison puts those events in perspective in his *History of United States Naval Operations in World War II, Vol. X, The Atlantic Battle Won:*

> The control of Atlantic sea lanes during World War II, insuring the safe, regular and frequent passage of ships, was but one link in the chain of forces and events that led to victory over the Axis.
>
> The challenge to Anglo-American-Russian shipping by the weaker German Navy offers a classic example of the futility of guerre de course (commerce raiding), and the triumph of the balanced fleet. Our Battle of the Atlantic is the best example in modern history of the value of strong sea and air power, skillfully and courageously applied.
>
> This battle opened with a bang on 3 September 1939, when U-30, in defiance of treaties to which Germany was a party, torpedoed and sank the unarmed and unescorted British passenger steamship Athenia. Before long, "no holds were barred," except what humanity and fear of reprisal dictated.

The future congressman's scornful opinion of a congressional fact-finding tour that came to Bremen was perhaps an
intimation of his later distaste for political junkets.

JULY 31, 1945

In Bremen the Forrestal team made an inspection of German
hardware and, according to JFK, had discussions with Navy
officials. Naturally, since JFK had served on PT boats in the
Pacific, which were of very poor design and durability, he was
interested to learn that the comparable German E boat was
of superior quality.

This fascination with how things were made and what
made them work was a trait that JFK showed throughout his
career. In his book *Let Us Begin Anew*, an oral history of the
Kennedy Administration, Glenn Seaborg, chairman of the
Atomic Energy Commission, confirms this fact. He reports
that the president asked to visit the commission headquarters
in February of 1961 and showed a sound technical grasp of
atomic and nuclear structure. Later, in December 1962,
President Kennedy asked Seaborg to arrange a visit for him
to the laboratory at Los Alamos; they traveled together in Air
Force One. At the site they went out to the crater by heli-
copter. According to the chairman the crater was "half a mile
across and maybe several hundred feet deep." The president
said to the pilot, "This is very interesting. Let's land in this
and look at it more closely." Seaborg and the pilot managed
to discourage the venture.

The total devastation of a nation by war, to the point where a nation's fate was measured in calories per day for subsistence, was unknown to Americans but very real in the Germany of 1945. Even stranger must it have been to Kennedy, insulated most of his life from mundane economic worries. The president's response to a reporter (Hugh Sidey, who revisits this incident in the Introduction to this volume) when asked if he had felt the Great Depression, was that the only major tragedy he had known was the war. JFK, perhaps because of his economic isolation, was always interested in finding out what things cost, how people lived, and what they earned.

The city of Bremen in 1945 had a population of 362,000. Bremen was a major industrial base for the Nazis in World War II and produced the bulk of their hardware for naval operations. The port city on the Weser River includes the shipbuilding area of Bremerhaven and is less than fifty miles from the North Sea. Bremen was heavily targeted during World War II, and more than half of its houses were destroyed.

During the spring of 1945 it took the Allied forces more than a week to secure Bremen. General Eisenhower, in his book *Crusade in Europe*, tells of General Montgomery's thrust to take the city:

> The eastward advance of the British Second Army, with three corps in the front line, reached the Weser April 5 and Elbe April 19. At Bremen the British Army encountered an enemy force determined to resist to the bitter end. The British 30 Corps reached the outskirts of the city April 20, but a week of bitter fighting was necessary before Bremen finally surrendered.

Eisenhower had to send additional help to support

Montgomery's drive into the city. General Ridgway's Airborne Corps joined the effort, and Bremen surrendered on April 26.

The reconstruction of a city like Bremen was a major undertaking for the military government management. There was less damage than in Berlin, but it was still necessary to rebuild public utilities, sanitary systems, and communications, as well as factories and homes. For these tasks manpower had to be trained and non-Nazis were required for all operations.

The military missions finance man, here in the diary interviewed by JFK, was a former director of a "small bank in the Mid-West." His job in handling the financial operations might be similar to a city manager in the U.S. He had to oversee the financial structure of the city, prevent black market operations, and restore the economic base.

JFK, with his constant inquisitiveness about how people lived, comments on the orderly ways of the hardworking Germans. He notes as he observes the countryside that trees "are considered a crop like corn." When Hugh Sidey and Senator Kennedy were flying into Cedar Rapids, Iowa, during the 1960 presidential campaign, the senator grilled reporter Sidey on the particulars of his home country by asking: "Hugh, how does it make you feel when you look down on your farm land? Does it bring back memories? I'm used to living in the Northeast and get a sense of magic when I go back to the ocean. Look at that soil, it looks good enough to eat! What about production costs, the price of the produce, what is it like to live on a farm, etc., etc."

AUGUST 1, 1945

The Forrestal party, including JFK, was met by General Eisenhower at the airport. In JFK's privately printed book in honor of his brother Joe, *As We Remember Him*, there is a photograph of General Eisenhower greeting Secretary Forrestal at the airport in Frankfurt on August 1. In the background is JFK.

We do know from the Forrestal papers in Princeton that, on August 1 at the Farben Building Eisenhower briefed Forrestal and JFK was there.

Frankfurt had become Eisenhower's headquarters in May of 1945. The I.G. Farben building was a luxurious office complex that had not been bombed out as had much of the surroundings.

Salzburg, Austria, on the German border and near the Northern foothills of the Alps, is one of the most beautiful cities in Europe. It is the birthplace of Mozart. From 1945 to 1956 it was the headquarters of the U.S. forces in Austria.

Berchtesgaden, the town across the border in Germany, and the site of Hitler's country retreat, "The Eagle's Nest," is located in a valley surrounded on all sides by Austria and the Alps. This picturesque area was used by the Allied occupation after World War II as a recreation spot. The building where the Forrestal party dined had been General Kietel's headquarters. Kietel was Field Marshall Wilhelm Kietel, the chief of the German high command.

The Nazi mountain retreats at Berchtesgaden, including air raid shelters and barracks, were heavily bombed by the Allies in April 1945. The ruins were leveled in 1952 to make way for a park. Forrestal and Kennedy would have been among the few to inspect the Eagle's Nest in its bombed-out and stripped-down condition. It is now a teahouse.

When JFK says that Hitler "had in him the stuff of which legends are made," he is speaking to the mystery surrounding him, not the evil he demonstrated to the world. Nowhere in this diary or in any of his writings is there any indication of sympathy for Nazi crimes, or the Nazi cause.

Appendix A

John F. Kennedy's Ten Favorite Books
(as given to Hugh Sidey in March 1961)

1. *Melbourne,* by David Cecil
2. *Montrose,* by John Buchan
3. *Marlborough,* by Winston Churchill
4. *John Quincy Adams,* by Samuel Flagg Bemis
5. *The Emergence of Lincoln,* by Allan Nevins
6. *The Price of Union,* by Herbert Agar
7. *John C. Calhoun,* by Margaret Coit
8. *Byron in Italy,* by Peter Quennell
9. *From Russia With Love,* by Ian Fleming
10. *The Red and the Black,* by M. deStendhal

Appendix B

Foreign Travel by John F. Kennedy up to the Time of Presidency*

1935

Summer	England—The London School of Economics.
October 17	Sickness—back to the U.S.

1937

	Trip to Europe with Lem Billings
July 1	Set sail on SS *Washington* bound for Europe. Docked in LeHavre, France. Traveled across tidal flats to Mont-Saint-Michel.
July 8	Soissons—saw the Chemin des Dames. Then to Reims—saw cathedral.
July 9	Fort Pompernelle.
July 10	Visited the Champagne caves of Pompernay. Went to Chateau Thierry.
July 13	Paris—Notre Dame. Lunched with Carmel Offie (American ambassador's secretary). Went to Versailles.
July 14	Visited the Louvre. Napoleon's Tomb and the Palace of the Invalids.

	Up the Eiffel Tower—then to Concierge where Marie Antoinette was kept. Back to U.S. embassy.
July 18	Explored Blois, then on to Chenonceau. Drove through Angouleme, through Tours to Poitiers. Stayed with Count de Pourtalis in St.-Jean-de-Luz.
July 24	Drove to Biarritz.
July 25	Attended high mass in church where Louis XIV married Marie-Therese. Drove to Spanish border—saw town of Irun.
July 27	Left the Pourtalises' and headed for Marseilles. Stopped at Lourdes—to look at grotto where the Virgin appeared to St. Bernadette. Left Toulouse and stopped at Carcassonne. Arrived at Cannes. Traveled to Monte Carlo.
August 1	Crossed border into Italy. Traveled down through Genoa to Milan. Saw Last Supper of Leonardo da Vinci. Drove down to Piacenza. Drove to Pisa—went through Tower of Pisa and the Baptistry. Arrived in Rome, went to the Coliseum.
August 5	Arrived in Vatican. Met with Cardinal Pacelli, Count Galeazzi—chief layman of the Catholic Church, Mr. Reed— counselor for the embassy. Saw St. Angelo Tomb of Hadrian, Pantheon, Coliseum.
August 7	Met privately with Cardinal Pacelli. Saw Pope with audience of 1,000. Went to Tivoli to see the fountains. Returned to Rome to have dinner with Count Galeazzi.
	Attended mass in St. Peter's and drove down to Naples. Drove to Vesuvius—drove up the rim of Mount Vesuvius. Traveled to Capri—went to the blue Grotto. Returned to Rome—visited Mr. Cortesi, the *New York Times* man in Rome.

	Attended a rally of Mussolini's in Rome.
	Shown through the Vatican museum.
August 12	Left Rome for Florence.
	Saw Michelangelo's David.
	Motored across Appenines, bound for Venice.
	While in Venice, saw Barbara Hutton and Al Lerner.
August 16	Traveled to Germany.
	Reached Brenner Pass.
	Started over the Alps to Germany.
	Stopped at Garmisch where Olympic Games were held, then on to Oberammagau.
August 17	Arrived in Munich. Went to the Hofbrauhaus, visited Deutsches Museum.
	Went to movie "Swing High, Swing Low."
	Visited Nuremburg.
	Left Nuremburg and set off for England via Frankfurt and the Rhine. Stopped off in Wurtemberg.
August 20	Went to Cologne by way of Frankfurt.
	Attended mass in Cologne cathedral.
	Headed for Utrecht. Went across the border into Holland.
	Went to Doorn, where kaiser lived.
	Arrived in Amsterdam—went to see Rembrandt's Night Watch.
	Arrived in Antwerp. Saw The Hague and beach at Ostend.
	Traveled to Calais—missed channel boat but made mail boat.
	Returned to London.
August 27	Went to Southampton to see his mother by train.
	Returned to London.
August 30	Visited Sir Paul Latham at Herstmonceaux Castle in Sussex.
	Went to see Sir James Calder in Kinrosshire, England. Returned to London.
September	Returned to Harvard.

1938

August	Spent summer vacation with family in Eden Roc in the South of France.
August 29	Returned to London with ambassador. Boarded SS *Bremen* at Southampton.
September 8	Arrived back in New York.

1939

February 24	Boarded *Queen Mary* with Ambassador Kennedy bound for England. Worked as assistant to his father, the ambassador.
	Met the king at Court Levee. Met Queen Mary and had tea with Princess Elizabeth.
March 12	Attended Pope Pius XII's coronation with Ambassador Kennedy, who was President Roosevelt's representative.
	Back to London with the ambassador.
	Went back to Paris with ambassador and had lunch with La Belle and Carmel Offie.
	Skied for a week in Switzerland. Had lunch with the Lindberghs.
April 8	Trip to Val D'Isere in France.
May	Departed for Danzig and the East. Stayed with Ambassador Biddle in Paris.
May	Traveled to Russia (Leningrad, Moscow, Kiev, and Crimea), Hungary, Lithuania, Latvia, Estonia, Rumania, Turkey, Palestine, and Egypt.
June 8	Departed for Bucharest, Hungary—returned via Beirut, Lebanon, Damascus, Athens, then London.
June 27	Attended a reception at 10 Downing Street hosted by Prime Minister Chamberlain.
July	With Torbert Macdonald traveled from England to France, Germany, Italy, and back to Paris.
	Met with "Whizzer" White in Munich in the Hofbrauhaus. Visited German countryside.

	Left London for Paris, Germany (Berlin and Munich), then to Italy, and back to Paris.
August	Drove to South of France where his mother had rented a summer home.
August 12	Left France for Germany. Drove to Munich, stayed one day, saw Tanhauser, and proceeded to Vienna. Went to Prague and then to Berlin.
Late August	Left Cannes, traveling through Germany to Czechoslovakia and Poland.
	While in Berlin briefed by Alex Kirk at the U.S. embassy in Berlin.
September 4	In the company of Kathleen, Joe Jr., his mother, and the ambassador, went to the Stranger's section of the House of Commons where, at noon, Prime Minister Chamberlain declared war.
September 6	Sent to Glasgow, Scotland, as ambassador's representative to those Americans who were aboard the SS *Athenia*, which had been sunk by German U-boat.
September 21	Arrived in New York to continue studies at Harvard.

1941

February	Recuperated in the Bahamas for several weeks.
May 7	Set sail aboard the *Argentina* with a destination of South America. Landed in Rio de Janeiro.
May 26	Flew to Argentina (spent two weeks). From Buenos Aires was escorted to Francisco de Vittoria, the Carcano family's ranch.
June 10	Flew to Montevideo, Uruguay. From there went to Santiago, Chile.
June 14	Boarded the USS *Santa Lucia*, bound for Valparaiso to New York. Made his way home via Peru, Ecuador, Colombia, and the Panama Canal.

1943

| February 11 | Dispatched to Jacksonville for duty in connection with |

the fitting of the Motor Torpedo Boat Squadron 14 (guard the Panama Canal).

March 6	Left from Pier 34 bound for the New Hebrides, north east of Australia.
April 1	Arrived in Espiritu Santo, in the New Hebrides.
April 3	Boarded transport landing ship that took him to Guadalcanal.
April 4	Began journey to Tulagi.
April 14	Arrived Sesapi, located on Tulagi's west shore, home of PT-boat headquarters in the Southwest Pacific.
December 21	Detached from duty in Motor Torpedo Boat Squadron 2.

1945

June	Visited ex-ambassador at Hyannis Port en route to England to cover the British elections for Hearst Newspapers.
July 23	Traveled to Ireland.
July 26	Flew to Paris to meet Secretary of the Navy Forrestal.
July 28	Flew to Berlin aboard Forrestal's plane as his personal guest. Arrived at Pottsdam.
July 29	Wandered through the ruins of Berlin with Secretary Forrestal and others.
July 30	Left Gatow Airport for Bremen and Bremenhaven.
July 31	Left Bremen for Frankfurt, then to Berchtesgaden.
August 1	Visited Hitler's mountain retreat, the Eagle's Nest.
August 2	Flew back to Washington with Secretary Forrestal.

1947

August 31	Flew from Boston to Shannon, Ireland.

Visited sister Kathleen at Lismore Castle on the Black Water River in County Waterford. Present at castle were Irish writer Charles Johnson, later British high commissioner to Australia; Hugh Fraser; Tony Rossyln, then a member of Parliament; and Anthony Eden, later prime minister.

September 21   Arrived in London (became extremely ill).

October 11   Arrived back in New York (via *Queen Mary*).

1951

Traveled as a member of the United States Senate.

January 9   Arrived in London.

Arrived in Yugoslavia and met with Marshall Tito.

January 30   Arrived in the Vatican. Visited Pope Pius XII, whom JFK had met earlier as Cardinal Pacelli.

Later in 1951

spent seven weeks in Asia.

---

* This list of travel may not be all-inclusive.

The following books were used as source material for this overseas travel:

Jack, The Struggles of John F. Kennedy
Herbert Parmet

JFK: Reckless Youth
Nigel Hamilton

The Search for JFK
Joan and Clay Blair

Appendix C

Facsimile of the Original Diary

Solved the *Missippi* course not [illegible]

"War is fatal to a democracy of both
..."
...

This war has been won — we have not
done our *utmost* & the *hands* of the enemy...

But It is still a question whether we shall *have*
won it in our *homes*. We have been
greatly weakened by this war — our *cause*
here has *done* a *work* [illegible] *welcome*
to *form* the *loss* of *unity* of *America* that
young men — many July on *age* [illegible]
the *leaders* of the *men* were so *deeply* *aroused*...

It is now & the *challenge* of the *present*
year. We *must* *show* for *past*
concern for *the* *our* *Year* of *the* *country* &
our *country* *than* *we have ever* *done* *in the*
past

School of instruction for lay catechists

Date Tu. 7 x 8 —   10   2°°   8 p

Topics — 1 hour — Christian social teaching.
          Appraisal of economic practices
              1 full employment
              2 — Housing
              3 — Wages
              4 — Encyclicals — talk formally

Quiz

day   afternoon   Guaranteed annual wage
                   Wages, prices & taxes —

             morning — Labor relations

Some Topics   Social security
               Pending legislation & laws

      afternoon — Problems facing field & workshop

      Evening — Stress ethics & pronouncements

Showing that the Church is not
national Catholic Welfare
Social Action Committee

Meeting of New England Mutual Health
to discuss — open to public
regardless of race creed or color

Rev. Dn. T. McCoughlin — Papers of
Sociology — Reports & Surveys

8 Water St.
St Vincent de
Paul

James Heeley

Conversation with Truman

Wants me to give money for _ Hamilton

7 Bureau. _____ situation

Studies are ones Truman failure to
get B. nai to come through.
B. nai notoriously stupid.

Thinks it will be popular thing in
time.

Remember Roosevelts principle that
you have to keep politicians & policies
apart.

Ed. Kelly the only really smart pres.
Pols can't tell what is going to happen.
B. nai situation will last for two more
months.

Truman is deader than Kelsey's
Nuts"

A file is going to follow things
depending on success of C.E.O

Water Cnuogg

Says 100 — bad politics

first press are more important

A, F L distinct

Laws govern later collective
bargaining + the power of red
strife

THE SAN FRANCISCO CONFERENCE

July 10, 1945

The Conference at San Francisco suffered from inadequate preparation and lack of fundamental agreement among the Big Three; from an unfortunate Press which praised it beyond all limit at its commencement which paved the way for subsequent disillusionment both in England and in this country.

The finished Charter is a product of these weaknesses — but it is also the product of the hope, and even more, the realization that humanity can ill afford another war.

In practice, I doubt that it will prove effective in the sense of its elaborate mechanics being frequently employed or vitally decisive in determining war or peace.

It is, however, a bridge between Russia and the Western world and makes possible discussion and a personal relationship which can do much to ease mutual suspicion.

The great danger is that the mechanism will not be employed; the trusteeship machinery will be used for only unimportant islands; the Social and Economic Body of the General Assembly will merely issue significant pamphlets on world conditions — significant in their content but not in their effect. And lastly, in far greater importance, because none of the larger countries will be willing, in the final analysis, to put the decision of war or peace in the hands of a delegate to a council, the Security Council will wither on the vine.

Instead, the Big Three meetings will continue to be called to settle ticklish problems -- which is good for temporary emergencies but a poor solution over long periods of time for it arouses distrust through the world and does not contribute to building a firm foundation for peace based on principle -- but rather makes a virtue of expediency.

As to the future, I do not agree with those people who advocate war now with the Russians on the argument "Eventually, why not now?" Fortunately, or unfortunately, depending on how you view it, democracies have to go through a gradual disillusionment in their hopes of peace; war must be shown to be the only alternative to preserve their independence -- or at least they must believe this to be true.

This was the great contribution of Neville Chamberlain who by giving Hitler every possible opportunity, shaming himself and indeed England to the world, finally convinced not only the Empire but even the United States that Germany was truly headed down the road to war. He made the way easy for his successor, Mr. Churchill, for he paved the eventual way for the entry of the United States into World War II. They were an admirable team - Mr. Churchill and Mr. Chamberlain - in securing our declaration, and of the two, I think that the latter did the most. He is given scant credit for it, particularly by the English people themselves, but perhaps history will be more generous.

I think that the clash with Russia will be greatly postponed. It will come perhaps, as its avoidance depends chiefly on the extent of Russia's self-restraint, and that is a quality of which powerful nations have a limited quantity.

The clash may be finally and indefinitely postponed by the eventual discovery of a weapon so horrible that it will truthfully mean the abolishment of all the nations employing it. Thus Science, which has contributed so much to the horrors of war, will still be the means of bringing it to an end.

If this is not done, the clash will take place -- probably involving first the British, perhaps in Persia, for the British are in great danger of sinking to a second-class power under the onslaught of Communism both in Asia and Europe. And they may prefer to fight rather than face it.

Tonight it looks like Labor and a good thing it
will be for the cause of free enterprise. The problems
are so large that it is right that Labor, which has
been nipping at the heels of private enterprise in England for the last twenty-five years, should be faced
with the responsibility of making good on its promises.

D--- maintains that free enterprise is the losing
cause. Capitalism is on the way out -- although many
Englishmen feel that this is not applicable to England
with its great democratic tradition and dislike of
interference with the individual.

I should think that they might be right in prosperous times, but when times go bad, as they must inevitably, it will be then that controls will be clamped on --
and then the only question will be the extent to which
they are tightened.

Socialism is inefficient; I will never believe
differently, but you can feed people in a socialistic
state, and that may be what will insure its eventual
success.

Mr. Roosevelt has contributed greatly to the end of
Capitalism in our own country, although he would probably argue the point at some length. He has done this,
not through the laws which he sponsored or were passed
during his Presidency, but rather through the emphasis
he put on rights rather than responsibilities - through
promises like, for example, his glib and completely impossible campaign promise of 1944 of 60,000,000 jobs.

He must have known that it was an impossibility to ever implement this promise, and it will hang as a sword over the head of a Capitalistic system — a system that will be discredited by its inability to make that promise good.

June 29, 1945

Kathleen and I went down this afternoon to Eastbourne in southern England to Compton Place. Eastbourne
is a small village and Compton Place is in the center
of it, though for its quietness it might be in the
middle of a large forest.

Its owner, the Duke of Devonshire, is an eighteenth-
century story book Duke in his beliefs - if not in his
appearance. He believes in the Divine Right of Dukes,
and in fairness, he is fully conscious of his obligations -- most of which consist of furnishing the people
of England with a statesman of mediocre ability but outstanding integrity.

David Ormsby-Gore maintains that in providing the
latter service the Aristocracy, especially the country
squires, really earn their sometimes extremely comfortable keep.

The Duke was a good friend of Neville Chamberlain.
He went on several fishing trips with him, but he said
that he could never understand Chamberlain's idea of
confiscating part of his land providing some "compensation" was made by the State. "But," said the Duke,
"what compensation can there be by handing over my
property to a middle-class official who can't administer
it half as well." And there you have the social philosophy of Edward, tenth Duke of Devonshire.

He had a number of interesting stories. One was
about Lady Violet Bonham-Carter, daughter of Herbert
Asquith, former Prime Minister.

Lady Violet had a great habit of bringing her face gradually closer and closer to the subject of her conversation until finally only several inches separated her from the recipient of her remarks. Duff-Cooper, Ambassador to France, finally became so infuriated with this habit that, at a dinner party, he suddenly picked up a potato with his fork and dashed it into her mouth saying, "Excuse me, I thought it was mine."

He was interesting on the subject of Napal -- an independent country from which the famous Ghurka warriors come. Great Britain was unable to conquer this principality so since the nineteenth-century conquest they have lived in peace with the Maharaja in close alliance.

The Ghurka soldier - crack troops - are mercenaries, who, being Moslems and therefore unable to cross the sea,have to go through an elaborate purification process before being allowed to enter their country after their tour of duty is complete.

Part of this purification process consists of bathing in cow urine and eating some cow manure.

As far as India on the whole, the Duke (Under-Secretary of State for Colonies) sees little hope for the future -- due to the terrific hostility of the Moslems and the Hindu's on the one hand and the completely mystic and debasing position of the 30 million "Untouchables." on the other. It is a poor foundation on which to build a democracy.

He admits, however, that England would also suffer if she were cut off completely from India, but the commercial ties are steadily becoming weakened by the

growth of Indian heavy industry and the influx of the
goods of other countries.

In the Levant, France had been consistently warned.
It was France's traditional policy of domination of
this part of the middle East which was carried out at a
time when French prestige and power was too weak to
successfully carry it through.

Although the Duke is an anachronism with hardly the
adaptability necessary to meet the changing tides of
present day, he does have great integrity and lives
simply with simple pleasures. He has a high sense of
noblesse oblige, and it comes sincerely for him. He
believes that Labor will win an overwhelming victory.
He is the only Conservative that I have heard state
this view.

His wife, grand-daughter of Lord Salisbury, Prime
Minister of England, is a woman of intense personal
charm and complete selflessness....................

hearts

General Eisenhower has taken a great hold on the ~~life~~ of all the British people. A typical story they tell: At the fall of Tunis in Africa back in 1943, a parade was held of all the forces that had brought the African campaign to a successful conclusion.

As the crack Eighth Army filed past, the Desert Rats, the Highland Division, the South Africans — all experiences and excellent troops — Eisenhower, as the supreme Commanding Officer, took the salute. He was heard to say after the Eighth had marched past, "To think that I, a boy from Abilene, Kansas, am the Commander of troops like those!" He never lost that humble way and therefore easily won the hearts of those with whom he worked.

Montgomery, on the other hand, while holding a unique position himself, won it the other way. Shortly before he went to take over the Eighth Army in the desert, Montgomery was heard to say, "A military career is a hard one — you win a battle and you are a hero — you lose one and you are disgraced."

The man with whom he talked said, "Cheer up, General, you should do well — you have good troops and fine equipment." "But," said Montgomery with some surprise, "I wasn't talking about myself, I was thinking of Rommell."

The Duchess said that the slaughter in the first war was extreme. Of seventy-five young men that she had known in 1914, seventy were killed in the war.

Churchill in his Book "World Crisis" brings out the same point — the terrific slaughter of the field officers of the British army - two or three times higher than the Germans. They were always on the defensive in the dark days of of '15, '16, and '17, and they paid most heavily.

The British lost one million of a population of forty million; the French, one million five hundred thousand of a population of thirty-eight million; and the Germans, one million five hundred thousand of a population of seventy million.

This tremendous slaughter had its effect on British policy in the '30's when Chamberlain and Baldwin could not bring themselves to subject the young men of Britain to the same horrible slaughter again.

NOTE: Churchill in his book "The Crisis" brings home with great force the amazing confidence and dependence that the British have put in their fleet as their number one line of defense.

July 1, 1945

I had dinner with William Douglas-Home, former
Captain in the British army, third son of Earl of
Home, cashiered and sentenced to a year in jail for
refusal to fire on   at LeHarve.

He is quite confident that his day will come after
his disgrace has passed, and he quotes Lord Beaverbrook
to the effect that some day he will be Prime Minister
to England. Like Disraeli he is extremely confident.

He feels that by insisting on the doctrine of
"Unconditional Surrender" instead of allowing Germany
and Russia both to remain of equal strength, we made
it possible for Russia to obtain that very dominance
that we fought Germany to prevent her having. He feels
that we had a great opportunity for a balance of power
policy.

For my own part, I think that only time can tell
whether he was right, but I doubt that William Home will
ever meet much success because people distrust those
who go against convention. And furth ermore, prowess
in war is still deeply respected. The day of the conscientious objector is not yet at hand.

(UPI/Bettman)

1. (Left to right) Eunice and Joseph P. Kennedy, Bishop James E. Cassidy, Rose and John F. Kennedy, John F. Fitzgerald (father of Rose), and Edward Kennedy.

John F. Kennedy Library

2. Joe Jr., Joseph P., and John F. Kennedy.

3. *JFK in London with his brother Joe Jr. and his sister Kathleen arriving at the special sitting of the House of Commons in London, September 1, 1939, as Parliament deliberated the action that eventually led to war.*

(AP/Wide World Photos)

4. Lady Hartington — JFK's sister Kathleen — chats with Randolph Churchill, son of Winston Churchill, at the American Independence Day party in London.

(AP/Wide World Photos)

(UPI/Bettman)

(UPI/Bettman)

5. *JFK, PT Boat Commander.*

6. *After receiving the Navy Marine Corps Medal.*

(Bettman Archives)

(UPI/Bettman)

7. At the Munich Conference (left to right): Chamberlain, Dalodier, Hitler, Mussolini, and Count Ciano(?). "They were an admirable team—Mr. Churchill and Mr. Chamberlain… and of the two, I think the latter did the most. He is given scant credit for it… perhaps history will be more generous."
—Kennedy, from his diary

8. Clement Attlee, leader of Britain's Labor Party, on his way to the "Big Three" conference.

(UPI/Bettman)

9. Harold Laski, Chairman of the Executive Council of the Labor Party. Kennedy discusses in his diary his impressions of a political rally he attended at which Laski spoke.

10. President Harry Truman (fifth from right, first row) poses with his military staff shortly before the final meeting of the "Big Three" in Potsdam. JFK was in Potsdam with Navy Secretary Forrestal at the time of the conference.

(UPI/Bettman)

11. Handshakes at a dinner given by Churchill for President Truman and Joseph Stalin in Potsdam.

12. Victory toast at Frankfurt on the Main. (Left to right) Bernard Montgomery of Britain, Eisenhower, Georgy Zhukov of the Soviet Union, and Arthur Tedder of Britain.

(UPI/Bettman)

(UPI/Bettman)

13. President Truman decorating Navy Secretary James Forrestal with the Medal of Merit. JFK accompanied Forrestal, a close Kennedy family friend, on his tour of Germany in 1945.

(UPI/Bettman)

(John F. Kennedy Library)

14. Forrestal (left) and Kennedy (second from right) in Berlin, 1945.

(Bettman Archives)

(UPI/Bettman)

15. Ruins of the Reichstag, Berlin, 1945.

16. Unter den Linden, Berlin, 1945. In the foreground is the empty skeleton of the Old Imperial Palace of the Kaiser. "The devastation is complete... there is not a single building which is not gutted."
—Kennedy, from his diary

17. Pierre Huss (left), Chief of the INS Bureau in Berlin, gets the inside scoop from American soldiers who had just infiltrated German lines.

18. Colonel Howley, Chief of American Military Government in Berlin.

(UPI/Bettman)

(UPI/Bettman)

19. *Heavy bombing of Berlin put water mains out of commission. People had to travel to working pumps and then boil water to avoid contamination.*

20. *"Where they are going, no one knows. I wonder whether they do."*

                                                        —*Kennedy, from his diary*

(UPI/Bettman)

21. *"During this winter the situation may be extremely severe."*
Kennedy, from his diary

22. *Berlin. "We drove...*
through miles of Russian soldiers. They were stationed on both sides of the road.... They looked rugged and tough, unsmiling but with perfect discipline."
—Kennedy, from his diary

(UPI/Bettman)

(Bettman Archives)

(Bettman Archives)

23 & 24. Hitler's Berchtesgaden chalet in the Bavarian Alps before allied bombing attacks.

(UPI/Bettman)

(UPI/Bettman)

25. *Berchtesgaden after being blasted by Allied bombs. "The walls were chipped and scarred by bullets, showing the terrific fight which took place at the time of its fall."*

— *Kennedy, from his diary*

26. *An awestruck U.S. soldier inspects the wreckage of the Berlin bunker where Hitler and Eva Braun reportedly died. "The room where Hitler was supposed to have met his death showed scorched walls and traces of fire. There is no complete evidence, however, that the body that was found was Hitler's body. The Russians doubt he is dead."*

— *Kennedy, from his diary*

(John F. Kennedy Library)

27. His war years behind him, Kennedy begins a long political career.

(UPI/Bettman)

28. *President Kennedy
meets with Assistant
Secretary of State W.
Averell Harriman.*

(UPI/Bettman)

29. *Ireland's President
Eamon de Valera greets
President Kennedy in
Dublin, Ireland.
Kennedy's early interest in
de Valera is evident in the
detail with which he dis-
cusses the Irishman in his
diary.*

(UPI/Bettman)

(John F. Kennedy Library)

(UPI/Bettman)

30. President Kennedy meeting with the Earl of Mountbatten (second from left), Chief of the British Defense staff; General Maxwell Taylor (left), Chairman of the Joint Chiefs of Staff; and close Kennedy friend British Ambassador to the United States David Ormsby-Gore (right).

31. (Left to right) Prime Minister Harold Macmillan; President Kennedy; David Ormsby-Gore, British Ambassador to the United States; Mrs. Kennedy; and Mrs. Ormsby-Gore, on the White House lawn, April 29, 1962.

32. President Kennedy in Palm Beach with Charles Bohlen, Ambassador to France.

(Time)

33. President Kennedy in the White House with Hugh Sidey, 1961.

(Deirdre Henderson)

34. Senator Kennedy with Deirdre Henderson, 1960.

July 2, 1945

The great danger in movements to the Left is that
the protagonists of the movement are so wrapped up with
the end that the means becomes secondary and things
like opposition have to be dispensed with as they obstruct the common good.

When one sees the iron hand with which the Trade
Unions are governed, the whips cracked, the obligatory
fee of the Trade Union's Political representatives in
Parliament, you wonder about the liberalism of the Left.
They must be most careful. To maintain Dictatorships
of the Left or Right are equally abhorrent no matter
what their doctrine or how great their efficiency.

I attended a political rally this evening at which Professor Harold Laski, Chairman of the Executive Council of the Labor Party and erstwhile Professor at the London School of Economics, spoke. He spoke with great venom and bitterness, and at the conclusion when asked if it were true that he wrote a letter to Mr. Attlee requesting him to resign as head of the Labor Party, he replied with asperity that it was "none of their business."

Odd this strain that runs through these radicals of the Left. It is that spirit which builds dictatorships as has been shown in Russia. I wonder whether a dictatorship of the Left could ever get control in England, a country with such a great democratic tradition. The next few years will answer that question.

These Leftists are filled with bitterness, and I am not sure how deeply the tradition of tolerance in England is ingrained in these bitter and discontented spirits. I think that unquestionably, from my talk with Laski, that he and others like him smart not so much from the economic inequality but from the social.

In speaking of Boston, he said, "Boston is a state of mind -- and as a Jew, he could understand what it is to be an Irishman in Boston." That last remark reveals the fundamental, motivating force of Mr. Laski's life -- a powerful spirit doomed to an inferior position because of his race -- a position that all his economic and intellectual superiority cannot raise him out of.

I left England yesterday to come to Ireland. World attention has been turned again to Mr. DeValera due to his recent remark in the "Irish Dail" that Ireland was a Republic. I stayed with Mr. David Gray, the American Minister to Ireland.

Mr. Gray's opinion of DeValera was that he was sincere, incorruptable, also a paranoiac and a lunatic. His premise is that the partition of Ireland is indefensable, and once this thesis is accepted, all else in its policy is consistent. He believed Germany was going to win. He kept strict neutrality even towards the simplest United States demand.

Mr. Gray admits that Mr. DeValera was not any more friendly to the Germans than he was to us. He does not think German submarines were aided from Ireland, at least with the knowledge of Mr. DeValera, although there were many German sympathizers.

He quoted the Cardinal in 1940 as having said that "he would take Germany as soon as England." The Cardinal believes that Ireland was created by God — a single island and people, and partition is therefore an offense to God. Gray says the island was maintained by the British during the war — gasoline, shoes, and coal — all were British.

He feels that the Civil War of 1921 was caused by the pride of DeValera. DeValera's constitutional proposals were very similar to those favored by President Cosgrave, Michael Dillon, and a majority of the "Dail." Yet, he split the country over the issue.

DeValera has a unique political machine. Only
one member of his caucas ever voted against him. He
has a way of bringing the national issue into every
question. He joined neutrality in this war with the
independence of Ireland. Either you were for neutrality and against partition or if you were against
neutrality you were for partition. As a Parliament
and political boss he is unique.

Gray admits he only caught DeValera once in the
"Dail? DeValera had made the statement that Ireland
had been completely blocked by Germany and England.
Mr. Gray proved him wrong. Gray feels that Ireland
should not attempt to become self-sufficient but rather
should become a highly intensified agricultural country.

Gray states that DeValera expected America and
England to follow out again at the end of this war
as they did at the end of the last war. If this had
happened, he would have been proved right. He did not
figure on Russia, which is now holding these two countries
together.

Churchill's speech at the end of the war, in which
he attacked DeValera, was extraordinarily indiscreet -
made things much more difficult for Gray and pulled
DeValera out of a hole.

James Dillon, in opposition to DeValera, believes
that far more could have been gotten by friendship with
Britain and by building mutual confidence. He feels
that DeValera is farther from their partition than when
he started.

Gray said that the Irish President's Secretary paid

a courtesy call on the German Legation at the time of
Hitler's death. He did not pay a call on the American
Legation at the time of Roosevelt's death. Now there
is a new President but O'Reilly, the Secretary, has
been kept on at the insistance of DeValera.

Gray says that of the 200,000 people who left
Ireland for England, only 30,000 joined the British
army in this war. In the first war 50,000 were killed
and 250,000 in service.

(End of talk with Gray)

DE VALERA

DeValera was born in New York, the son of a Spanish father and Irish mother. He took part in Sir Roger de Casement's Rebellion in 1916, which through lack of German help was unsuccessful. The Revolutionists seized the city for a week but were finally overpowered by the British.

At this time they had little public support as the British had successfully imposed a complete blackout on news.

The leaders were jailed, and in order to impress the populous, the British commenced to shoot their leaders — one or two a day. DeValera was comparatively unknown and therefore near the end of the list, and because public indignation had come to a fever pitch in America and Ireland due to the daily executions, the British reprieved DeValera and removed him to an English jail.

There he was confined until he finally arranged his escape. He took some wax from the altar where he was serving Mass, made an impression of a key, and had one of his companions draw a Christmas card showing a drunk coming home from a Christmas party trying to put a very large key into a very small key hole. Another drawing showed another drunk coming home trying to put a very small key into a very large key hole. This card was sent to his friends in Ireland where it lay around for several months before one day someone picked it up and realized what it was.

Michael Collins, the great Irish hero, arranged for keys to be sent to DeValera in jail in a cake and went to England himself to aid the escape. One of the keys broke but at the last minute Mr. DeValera was successful in breaking out.

He was met by Collins and smuggled across to Ireland and thence to the United States where he argued sympathy for Ireland's fight for freedom at the end of the war against the Black and Tans. He returned to Ireland and broke with Collins and Cosgrave over their acceptance of a treaty with Great Britain. Thought Collins was killed, DeValera was defeated, and since that time he has fought politically in the "Dail" the same battle that he fought militarily in the field -- a battle to end partition, a battle against Great Britain.

He came to power eventually in 1932 over the question of annuities - the money that the Irish were paying to the British for the land that had been taken from the landlords and given to the Irish peasants.

Mr. DeValera opposed these payments, and the peasants who would have had to pay 50 per cent of this sum supported him strongly because it pleased both their pocketbook and their independent capitalistic spirit.

England retaliated by setting a tariff on every head of cattle shipped to England. This tariff had to be paid by Ireland to keep its market. This was a great financial loss to Eire, and the matter was finally settled after a long economic war byan outright payment of $10,000,000 cash. This, combined by the money paid by tariff, came to a greater amount than the annuities had been in the first place.

Because of DeValera's appeal to nationalism and his mystic hold on the hearts of the people and his practical politics, he did not lose control.

Ireland was in a poor condition at the end of this economic war as nearly 200,000 cows were slaughtered because of the British tariff.

FINANCE

Ireland receives about $4,000,000 a year from the United States in remittances as she needs about $15,000,000 more to pay for her imports. Her dollar exchange has been given her by England. This put Ireland in a position of independence.

Many Irishmen feel that it a great mistake to be so closely tied up with the sterling bloc. It is bondage they claim.

England has many weapons with which she could strangle Ireland — a tariff on beef, shutting off her credit, as well as the use of force. England so far has done remarkably in practicing self-restraint, but Gray believes that on its previous form it will probably make some serious error in the future.

(Note:) Sheridan once said, "The quarrel is a very pretty quarrel as it stands; we should only spoil it by trying to explain it."

(Note:) A thought for Irishmen abroad — written by Thomas D'Arcy McGee, a Canadian of Irish birth.

"Our first duty is to the land where we live and have fixed our homes; and where, while we live, we must find the true sphere of our duties. While always ready therefore to say the right word and do the right act for the land of my forefathers, I am bound above all to the land where I reside."

IRELAND

The two chief parties of Ireland are the Fine Gael (United Ireland Party) and the Fianna Fail - the "soldiers of Ireland Party."

The former is led by General Mulcahy and was organized by William Cosgrave. It is always believed that the way to end partition is to cooperate with the British - not fight them.

The Fianna Fail, now the most powerful party in Ireland, is DeValera's party which came into power in 1930. Both these parties are fighting the same political battle in the "Doil" that they fought in the Civil War.

What has weakened Cosgrave's party is that DeValera who has bitterly opposed Great Britain was the party that ended British control of the ports -- a concession that Great Britain was unwilling to give Mr. Cosgrave in spite of his sincere desire to cooperate.

This has given DeValera ammunition and has given some substance to his feeling that everything that has ever been gotten by Ireland from England has been given grudgingly and at the end of a long and bitter battle.

Seventy per cent of the Irish population is on the land. This gives the population a very conservative out-look.

When a politician in Ireland speaks of the "Left" he is not referring to its attitude towards national industry but rather its attitude towards the Republic and the ending of partition. The Left is the anti-British group - the Right those in favor of working out a compromise.

DeValera in his efforts to make this island self-sufficient and lessen its dependence on Great Britain has raised the wheat acreage from 20,000 to 200,000 from 1932 to 1944.

This may increase its economic self-sufficiency, but wheat is not a profitable product for misty, rainy Ireland to grow.

IMPRESSION OF BRITISH ELECTION RESULTS

The overwhelming victory of the Left was a
surprise to everyone. It is important in assaying
this election to decide how much of the victory was
due to a "time for a change" vote which would have
voted against any government in power, whether Right
or Left, and how much was due to real Socialistic
strength.

My own opinion is that it was about 40 per
cent due to dissatisfaction with conditions over
which the government had no great control but from
which they must bear responsibility -- 20 per cent
due to a belief in Socialism as the only solution to
the multifarious problems England must face -- and
the remaining 40 per cent due to a class feeling -
i.e.; that it was time "the working man" had a chance.

For too long a time now England has been de-
vided into the two nations as Disraeli called them --
the rich and the poor.

The Labor Party will stay in for a long time
if the conservative wing of that party -- men like
Attlee and Bevin remain in office.

But if the radical group like Laski, Shinwell,
and Cripps become the dominating influence in the
party, there will be a reaction and the Conservatives
will come once again to power. In my own opinion
Attlee will remain in office for the next year and a
half, but if there is much dissatisfaction, which there
well may be, he will go; and as a sop to the radical

Left wing, Morrison or Bevin will take over.

Labor is laboring under the great disadvantage of having made promises to numerous groups whose aims are completely incompatible. The Conservatives may pick up some of these votes, at least those of the middle class when conditions make it impossible for Labor to implement many of its promises.

Some Figures which Emphasize Britain's Problems

Only by being highly organized by government directives can Britain grow as much as 2/3 of the food necessary to feed her population.

In 1938:

Britain consumed imports of
858,000,000 pounds

The government made payments overseas of
13,000,000 pounds

Total
871,000,000 pounds

Export of merchandise
471,000,000 pounds

Income from overseas investments
200,000,000 pounds

Net shipping earnings   200,000,000 pounds

Misc.   35,000,000 pounds

Revenue   806,000,000 pounds

Deficit   65,000,000 pounds

Total external debt of Great Britain in 1945 is 5,000,000,000 pounds of which the India debt is 1,000,000,000 pounds.

Notes on France

People are disappointed with DeGaulle. He has not pleased any group (which may be a sign of fair government) and has made himself extremely unpopular with most. Any movement against DeGaulle will take the form of a swing to the Left — the victory of the Socialists in Britain may accentuate this swing.

Food is hard to get for people in the city because of lack of transportation. This lack of transportation has contributed greatly to the difficulties all throughout Europe.

United States unpopularity is strengthened by the fact that we control most of the rolling stock (railroad, cars, trucks, etc.) and use it to feed and supply our own forces. The French have nothing.
Monetary:

The Franc is stabilized at 50 to the dollar. This is an artificial rate — the actual ratio is nearer 150 to the dollar. This gives the French a bonus as prices are on the 150 Franc ratio scale and our troops are paid at the 50 to the dollar ratio. Importers into France, of course, have an advantage under this setup, but exporters who are attempting to sell brandies and wines are at a substantial disadvantage.

The French plan for a capital levy is extremely interesting and may prove a precedent for other countries in Europe and eventually throughout the world.

The present plan is for the government to take over 5 per cent of the stock and sell it to the public, keeping the profit for themselves.

This may be done up to 20 per cent.

Note:

Perfumes and other luxury goods are no longer of first-class quality. Perfumes are not the musk base of former days. The musk supply, which comes from the East, has been turned off.

GERMANY

With Secretary of the Navy Forrestal and others of his party, we left Paris at about three o'clock in the Secretary's C54 plane for Berlin.

In flying over Germany, the small towns and fields looked peaceful, but in the larger cities like Frankfort the buildings are merely of the sods. All the centers of the big cities are of the same ash gray color from the air — the color of churned up and powdered stone and brick. Railroad centers are especially badly hit, but the harvest seems to be reasonably good and the fields appear as though they were being worked fully.

At the field at Berlin where we arrived, Prime Minister Attlee came in just ahead of us. There was a large crowd, and he inspected the same Guard of Honor which Prime Minister had inspected only a few days before. We drove immediately to Potsdam through miles of Russian soldiers. They were stationed on both sides of the road at about 40 yard intervals -- green-hatted and green-epauleted -- Stalin's personal and picked guard. They looked rugged and tough, unsmiling but with perfect discipline. As the cars drove by, they presented arms.

We stopped in front of the President's house which was in a peaceful Potsdam square untouched by war. It was small but surrounded by our own M.P.'s, evidently influenced by the Russians because they saluted and stood at attention like Marines.

Here, as in all the rest of Germany, the
Army discipline was perfect — a far cry from the
laxity of Paris. Outside of the President's house
were the plain-clothes men of the American Secret
Service. They looked big and tough and equally as
unsmiling as the Russians.

The Secretary talked to the President for a
few minutes, and then we drove to a house on the
Kleine Wann See -- a beautifully furnished house
on a wonderful location along a beautiful lake.
It was untouched by bombs, but during the evening
as we drove along the lake in a speed boat, many of
the houses in this residential section were badly
hit.

Notes:

The Russian Army in Berlin now is the second
Russian Army to be in occupation. The first army,
which was the fighting army, had been withdrawn by
the time we arrived. The Russians gave the first
army a 72-hour pass after they had taken the city,
and raping and looting was general. What they didn't
take, they destroyed. When that army had been withdrawn, the second Russian Army was given the same
leave and the same privileges, but since that time
the discipline has been better. The Russians have
been taking all the able-bodied men and women and
shipping them away. Prisoners that we released are
taken up and sent back to Russia.

All the children under fifteen or women over
fifty and old men are dumped into the American zone
and thus become an American responsibility.

(Feeding)

There are approximately 900,000 originally
in the American zone. The French have been added
to the occupation forces at the expense of the
British who now have 200,000 fewer to feed. But it
means that the Americans now have 200,000 extra
mouths to feed as the Americans are supplying food
for the French district.

(Note)

There seems to be a general feeling here
that the Germans hoped that the German Army would
stop fighting in the West and permit the Allies to
come in before the Russians. As far as the Russian
treatment of the Germans, most admit that it was as
bad as the propaganda had told them it would be.
Raping was general. The Russians stole watches in
payment and cameras were second choice. The Russians
have recently been paid and they are very free with
their money. The standard price for watches brought
some Americans over $400. The official rate of ex-
change is 10 marks to the dollar.

One opinion here is that the Russians are never going to pull out of their zone of occupation but plan to make their part of Germany a Soviet Socialist Republic. The question, therefore, is whether the other three occupying forces can afford to leave their zones. So far, the British seem to be encouraging a German economic revival. (The new British government may change this.)

The French who are in the Rhine area will probably want to continue to take large portions of German production. The United States will probably want to pull out -- the present plan is to keep an occupying army of 400,000. If a split among the Big Four develops as far as long-time administrative procedure, it will be serious. Germany will be unable to build and maintain communications, roads, canals, trade, coal, and food. If we don't withdraw and allow them to administer their own affairs, we will be confronted with an extremely difficult administrative problem. Yet, if we pull out, we may leave a political vacuum that the Russians will be only too glad to fill.

Impressions of Berlin Ruins ———————

The devastation is complete. Unter der Linden
and the streets are relatively clear, but there is
not a single building which is not gutted. On
some of the streets the stench —— sweet and sickish
from dead bodies —— is overwhelming.

The people all have completely colorless
faces —— a yellow tinge with pale tan lips. They
are all carrying bundles. Where they are going, no
one seems to know. I wonder whether they do.

They sleep in cellars. The women will do anything for food. One or two of the women wore lipstick, but most seem to be trying to make themselves
as unobtrusive as possible to escape the notice of
the Russians.

The Russians were short, stocky, and dour
looking. Their features were heavy and their uniforms dirty,

Hitler's Reich Chancellery was a shell. The
walls were chipped and scarred by bullets, showing
the terrific fight which took place at the time of
its fall. Hitler's air-raid shelter was about
120 feet down into the ground - well furnished but
completely devastated. The room where Hitler was
supposed to have met his death showed scorched walls
and traces of fire. There is no complete evidence,
however, that the body that was found was Hitler's
body. The Russians doubt that he is dead.

On our arrival in Berlin, the American group
was viewed with profound distrust. The Russians did
not let them take over for the first few days using
as their excuse — that they had to have time to
evacuate. The Col. thinks, however, that it was because they wanted to continue their looting.

The Colonel ordered his staff to move in one
morning. When the Russians arrived at their offices,
they found the Americans already there. After a few
protests, they retired. Now things are working
reasonably smoothly.

All decisions have to be unanimous between the
four occupying powers. They run the city as a unit —
they work disputes over until the decision is unanimous.

Up until now the food for the American zone
is delivered by the Americans to the edge of the
Russian zone in the West, which extends 200 miles
west of Berlin. Then the Russians transport it to
Berlin. After August fifteenth, when the bridges
and roads are fixed, the United States will bring
their food in directly.

The basic ration is 1½ pounds a day – approximately 1,200 calories (2,000 considered by the health
authorities for normal diet – the ration is only 900
calories in Vienna)

The British ship in about 9,000 tons of coal
a day for the city which is used for public utilities
and for the services of the occupying forces. During
this winter the situation may be extremely severe.
The Colonel thinks that the Russians may be hard pressed.
If they are, they undoubtedly will take the food meant
for the civilians. This may present a problem for us
because the Americans cannot feed their civilians
better than those in the Russian zone because this
would cause an influx from all over Berlin.

The Russians have pretty well plundered the
country, have been living off it - and therefore,
although they control the food basket of Germany,
they may never be able to develop their quota for
this winter.

The Russian staff work, according to the Colonel,
is sloppy. When they make appointments, they may not
keep them. Ordinarily, this is not due to indifference
to the Americans but merely because they are home drunk
in bed. The Colonel says that Americans have to talk
tough and know their facts. He does feel, however,
that the suspicion between the Russians and the Americans
has lessened since the occupation began.

Talk with Pierre Huss,
Chief of the INS Bureau of Berlin

The Russians moved in with such violence at
the beginning -- stripping factories and raping
women -- that they alienated the German members of
the Communistic Party, which had some strength in
the factories.

German Communists protested to Zhukov, who
has now moved in another Army, the show army, and
the Russians are now allowing political activity
though strictly controled. There are four political
parties - all left wing - and the Russians are going
to bring back the Paulus Committee from Moscow which
they hope may be able to rally the powerful old families.
(This looks like a dubious hope to me.)

The Russians are putting it over us as far as
political activity goes -- they have opened the schools,
they are publishing papers -- we have done none of
these things. We seem to have no definite policy.

I feel myself that the Russians have a long way
to go before they can erase the first terrible impression
they made on the Berliners. Therefore, any political
activity which is backed directly by Moscow will have
great difficulty in meeting much public support among
the Germans.

Conversation with a German Girl

This girl is about twenty-two, speaks some
English, and is a Roman Catholic. She said it was
difficult to get to Catholic church after the Nazis
came to power, though it was possible. She thought
the Germans were going to win the war but the first
victories were just "shiny."

She thought the future of Germany is "melancholy."
After finishing her secondary school education, she
worked for a year doing manual labor. The work was
extremely hard. She then returned to the University
and as the war got increasingly severe, she went to
the western front and worked with a search-light crew.
She felt that the war was lost in 1942 when American
planes came over.

When the Russians came, she and her two sisters
were taken down to the cellar. Her clothes were "taken
out" - she gave them all her rings, cried, waved a
bottle of wine. Her "face was blue." She demonstrated
by swinging a bottle at me. I can quite believe that
no Russian would want to rape her. She says the
Russians let them go untouched. When the Russians saw
the Holy Mother's picture and the Crucifix on the wall,
they said, "You must be anti-Nazi if you're a Catholic."

People did not realize what was going on in
the concentration camps. In many ways the "SS" were as
bad as the Russians. The feeding in Berlin was extremely well organized, even in the most severe blitz.

Her brother was killed on the Eastern front and

her fiance is in an Italian prisoner-of-war camp.
She feels that Russia and the United States will
fight when Russia is ready, They now know that our
equipment is far superior.

She feels that that war would be the ruination
of Germany which would be the common battleground.

Note:

SS was enlarged in 1942 because Himmler wanted
to increase his own power. Their brutality was,
therefore, diluted by forced recruits.

Note:

According to our naval experts, the bombing of
Germany was not effective in stopping their production
and production increased three-fold during 1942-44.

Note:

                                                    in Berlin
One of the debatable questions now/is whether
Berlin will ever be built up again into a large city.
If Germany remains divided into four administrative
units as she is now, Berlin will remain a ruined and
unproductive city. In any case, it will be many years
before Berlin can clear the wreckage and get the material
to rebuild.

Bremen

Arrived in Bremen from Berlin in the morning.
Met at airport by Rear Admiral Robinson, former
Commander of the Marblehead. Had lunch and then went
to Bremershaven – a large port on the North Sea which
is now filled with many ships including the Europa.

The countryside surrounding Bremen is beautiful
and the crops were abundant. Cattle, sheep, and
chickens were numerous. (The Dutch and French claim
that they were stolen from them.)

The people were fat and rosy, completely unlike
the anemic, shocked, and frightened Berliners. There
was little evidence of war – no bomb damage. This area
will do well this year.

The harbor of Bremershaven was full of captured
ships. The Europa was getting up steam as we drove
in and should be ready to leave in another month. for
America to be converted into a troop transport. She
still has aboard her old Captain and some of the crew
who were with her when she was making her old transatlantic runs. He was captured by the British on a
raid on Narvik, was interned in Canada, and repatriated
in 1944, and has been on the ship ever since. They may
keep him aboard with many of the old engineers, as they
are skilled, speak English, and do not seem to have had
close Nazi connections.

From there we went to a gigantic new construction intended for a Willow Run type of submarine production, the submarines to be produced at the rate of one every two days. It was over 400 yards long, 100 yards wide, and 70 yards high. The concrete on the roof was 14 feet thick, and although one bomb had pierced it, the roof due to its extremely clever design was nearly intact. They were getting ready to double the thickness of the roof which would have been an architectural and engineering masterpiece when the war ended. Construction is being pushed on this building right up to the war's end.

From there we went to a ship-yard where they were assembling pre-fabricated submarines. The parts were assembled in the South and East and the sections were brought by barges along the canals and assembled here. The bombing had not damaged any of the 24 submarines along the water's edge, although the wreckage was heavy about a quarter of a mile in shore. The British seem to have concentrated and bombed only the machine and tool shops.

Figures were given which showed German submarine production at about one a day. 11,000 were launched from 1939 to 1945, and Forrestal said 600 had been sunk.

These submarines were all equipped with the Schozzle breathing device which enabled them to stay under water for long periods. One submarine on a 30-day cruise only surfaced four hours.

Because of unusual hull design and double-sized batteries, they could go at far greater speed under water than we could attain - approximately 18 knots - while being relatively slow on the surface (the reverse of ours).

Their living quarters were extremely bad. U. S. cruisers would never have stood for them.

We then drove through the bombed out section of Bremen. The devastation was acute, although the space along the docks (the cranes, etc.) was undamaged. The people, however, looked very well, full of health, and well-fed. They had none of that pinched, hurrying look of the Berliners.

They get no coal, however, and their present diet from us is about 1,200 calories - ours being 4,000. However, they have large reserves which they can draw on.

The fraternization is as frequent as in Berlin. People do not seem to realize how fortunate they have been in escaping the Russians. As far as looting the homes and the towns, however, the British and ourselves have been very guilty.

In spite of the apparent well-being of the people, however, there still remains the question "How well will they do this winter?"

Note:

The Congressional Committee under Luther Johnson came through here on a fact-finding tour. According to the Naval personnel, all they were interested in were lugers and cameras.

July 31, 1945

Spent the day in Bremen talking to Navy officials
and to the heads of military government in this area.

Among other things, the Navy had accurate reports on German E boats which correspond to our PT
boats. The German boat was approximately 105 feet -
engines developed 6,000 horse power - had four torpedo
tubes and a gun equivalent to our 40 mm - a couple of
20 mm's and some light machine guns.

In speed they ranged from 42 knots to 49 knots
in actual trials. Their cruising range was about 700
miles at 35 knots - their displacement about 115 tons -
their engines were Diesel.

These figures demonstrate that the German E boat
was far superior to our PT boat. It was 25 feet longer,
just as fast, nearly twice as heavy, and had greater
cruising range at high speed - in armament it was about
equal. Their boat is a better heavy-water boat, cheaper
to operate because it burns oil instead of gasoline -
and for the same reason, safer from fire or explosion.

The officials in the military government seemed
most efficient and sensible in their approach.
Evidently, Bremen and Berlin draw the top teams. They
were employing Germans as much as possible after first
weeding out the party members. They found the Germans
extremely willing, almost docile in accepting directions.
They had a passion for accuracy, and they had an involved price and wage scale which was thorough and worked
well.

In this connection, the Army released several prisoners who had three-year sentences for killing one of their pigs without government permission.

The chief of our government mission felt that the present ration of 1,200 calories was insufficient; it bred hunger and led to black markets (of which at present there were only a few) and dissatisfaction and made their task that much more difficult.

He hoped to get the schools opened by September up to the eighth grade but anticipated difficulty in securing the proper teachers as most of the old ones were strong Nazis. As far as the percentage of Nazis in the town, it was about 5 per cent.

The city of Bremen was a port city and, therefore, dependent on the surrounding country, much of which was under British control for its food.

The British had been extremely cooperative as far as exchanging food-stuffs. So far little food in this area had been sent to the relief of Berlin, but they were planning to send some dried fish that they had taken from the Germans.

The British had gone into Bremen ahead of us - and everyone was unanimous in their description of British looting and destruction which had been very heavy. They had taken everything which at all related to the sea - ships, small boats, lubricants, machinery, etc.

The military missions finance man was a
former director of a small bank in the Mid-West.
He was an intelligent man and seemed in every way
to be excellent for the job. He said that all financing for the Occupations and for the repair of ships
was being paid for by the city of Bremen and the
Reichsbanks local branch.

Figures:

The amount on hand at time of occupations held by
city of Bremen - *72,000,000 R. Marks (securities, etc.)
Amount on hand at time of occupations in Reichs
tax office -   21,000,000 Marks
The cost of American occupations to this date
(repair of ships, labor pay) 1,600,000 marks
of which Reich tax office paid 1,000,000 marks
The City of Bremen   600,000 marks
Income from first three months of fiscal year of Reich
tax office (April, May, and June of 1944 - 32,000,000 marks
In same period for 1945 -   2,500,000 marks
                                              ≠ 8%

* Reichsmarks in value as far as labor pay and price
is equivalent to 2½ Reichsmarks to the dollar.

He found that Germans were good workers, the
bureaucratic administration setup in the town of
Bremen was complicated but efficient with municipal
ownership that was wide-spread.

People had commenced paying taxes and the city
was being run as nearly as possible as before - with
the same wages being paid.

He found that there seemed to be no central
plan among our officers. Some treated Germans as a
conquered people and got bad results. He believed in
treating them as any other employee and found in that
way he got the best work. He said that there were as
yet few black markets but they should increase during
winter. Like everyone else he said that the coal
shortage was acute. People were cutting wood to heat
their food but in the winter the Germans would be in
a desperate situation.

Notes:

    A. Americans looted towns heavily on arrival.

    B. American plan seems to be to get things
       started so that the Germans can look out
       for themselves; to remove all those with
       Nazi connections (this in some cases re-
       moves the most efficient administrators)
       and to try to keep Germany divided into
       separate administrative units.

    C. The people looked well here and reasonably
       cheerful - a great change from Berlin.

D. None of the officers and men here seem to have
any particular hate for the Germans, although some
throw their weight around.

E. I am quite surprised to see with what zest the
German girls, who can be very attractive, throw themselves at the Americans. I cannot believe it would
be this way in England or America if the situation
were reversed. They argue that there haven't been
any men around for four years and it is merely
biological.

F. Passing over the German countryside one sees
rows and rows of trees, all in orderly groups of
different sizes. Trees obviously are considered a
crop as much as corn. We could learn a lesson from
that in conservation.

G. The docility of the German bureaucrats demonstrates
how easy it would be to seize power in Germany. They
have not the inquisitive minds of the Americans and
the instinctive "I'm from Missouri" attitude towards
authority.

We flew from Bremen to Frankfurt and were met
at the airport by a Battalion of Paratroopers and
General Eisenhower. The troops were as well drilled
as any I have seen. In fact, all the troops that I
have seen in Germany have been outstanding.

We drove to the Farber building which was completely untouched, though surrounded by ruins.
Eisenhower talked with Forrestal for a few minutes,
and it was obvious why he is an outstanding figure.
He has an easy personality, immense self-assurance,
and gave an excellent presentation of the situation
in Germany.

He said that the situation was complicated by
the fact that the Russians in the East have the major
food-producing area in Germany while the British,
French, and United States in the West were strong on
steel, coal, iron, and the manufacturing centers but
were deficient in food.

The British section was about 40 per cent self-
sufficient -- we in the South were about 70 per cent
self-sufficient. This economic diversification of
Germany is what caused Bismark in 1870 to unite
Germany into one unit, which by nature it is. The
same factors are facing those people who advocate the
breaking up of Germany into old principalities.

In Frankfurt deep underground in the salt mine
was found nearly $300,000,000 in gold, silver, securities,
and other loot. There was gold from Hungary and France.
France is claiming most of it.

There were securities from France and the other countries of the world. We visited it and it was piled brick on brick - bag on bag - in the cellar of the Reichsmark. Its ultimate disposal is still un-decided.

Note:

So far, there has been no negotiation with the Russians about how much Occupation money will be printed. They have been printing marks wholesale in Berlin, they pay 4,000 marks for a watch which we have been cashing in at the rate of 10 for a dollar.

From Frankfurt we flew to Salzburg, where
King Leopold was detained, and drove to the town of
Berchesgarden. It is a beautiful town in the mountains -
the houses are alpine in architecture, and the people
are well-fed and healthy. There is no bomb damage and
there is plenty of wood to take the place of coal. It
is a town apart from the destruction of war. We
stayed at a beautiful inn for the evening after dining
with the local General at the lavishly furnished
building that was formerly the headquarters of General
Kietal. It was reported that there were six miles of
corridors underneath the main building.

The dinner consisted of about six courses -
Rhine wines and champagne. After dinner they brought
out some cigars taken from Goering's armored car.

In the morning we went up to Hitler's mountain
home. It was completely gutted, the result of an air
attack from 12,000 pound bombs by the R·A·F. in an
attempt on Hitler's life.

Leaving the chalet, we drove to the very top
of the mountains (about 7,000 feet) where the famed
Eagle's lair was located. The road up was covered
with solid rock in many places and was cleverly camouflaged. On arrival at the top, we entered a long tunnel
carved through the rocks and came to an elevator which
took us up through solid rock for the last 600 feet.
The elevator was a double-decker - a space being left
on the lower deck for the SS guard.

The lair itself had been stripped of its rugs,
pictures, and tapestries, but the view was beautiful –
the living room being round and facing out on every
side on the valley below.

After visiting these two places, you can easily
understand how that within a few years Hitler will
emerge from the hatred that surrounds him now as one
of the most significant figures who ever lived.

He had boundless ambition for his country
which rendered him a menace to the peace of the world,
but he had a mystery about him in the way that he
lived and in the manner of his death that will live
and grow after him. He had in him the stuff of which
legends are made.

Jan. 27 —

Conversation with Dan O'Brien

Says I'll get murdered —
his practical experience —
a personal observation. Says
I don't know 300 people
personally — says I shall
become him himself
Say x

O'Brien indicates the
attack on me will be
1. Inexperience.
2. Trying to rule me in
my father reputation.

He is the first man
to say that I can't win!
An honest Irishman but

a mistake me

In politics you don't
have friends — you have
confederates

One day they feed you honey —
the next day they will find
fault with your throat.

You can buy brains but
you can't buy loyalty

Plant — humble

Singer, McClurg — Philadelphia

Ireland & the Pres of the U.S

John Reagan — 4518.323.1

Ireland & S.A.
    Patrick   William Morris
            355 9.131

* Ireland in America" — E184,
    R Edward E Serguin   . E627

Ireland the world over — * D.A 913
            . W 33

Ireland Contribution to law —
    Hugh Carney   2418.45

Irish-American Hist of the U.S
    John O'Hanlon   2 321.115

Irish Confederation –
4414.335
Thomas Maguinness

The Irish American

Bryan Burnett

No 1 in + 4511.103

The Irish in America

Thomas Bowd. 4317.31

Irish in America

James Farley - no 6 in

4226.491

Mooreped ff ney -

American of Irish Lineage

451.M.281

Irish in U.S - DA919.W37

George Welleton

New England left DA578

.K4

Thomas Walsh

J A 925 · W3

✓ Wh...

World's Law & the Press

"The ...ast politician is the
man who does not think to
much of the political consequences
of his every act".

Jarly
Democratic party has ...
became — Wilson — "it had a
heart under its jacket"

"The no great ... in American gov't
is the gov't of cities.

Mr. Bruce — America Commonwealth

Harry Pokat
251 Chamber St.
West End

Shipping Companies — the company non-permanent
employer
10 years — workers of Ocean Steamship —
Formerly a Long-shoreman — Union

James P. O'Brian
231 Lexington Ave
Cambridge Eli 1285

Joseph L. Riordon Reardon
30 Aberdeen Ave
Cambridge — Eli 0472

ACKNOWLEDGMENTS

With deep thanks for their sound professional counsel to Michael F. Robinson, Molly H. Sherden, and Andrew W. Smart. Thanks to the Cambridge Public Library, Collins Branch, and the John F. Kennedy Library, Boston, Massachusetts, for access to their books and documents, and to Daniel Garvey, research assistant.

BIBLIOGRAPHY

Abramson, Rudy. *Spanning the Century: The Life of W. Averell Harriman, 1891–1986.* New York: William Morrow and Company, Inc.

Ayer, Fred Jr., *Before the Colors Fade: Portrait of a Soldier, George S. Patton, Jr.* Boston: Houghton Mifflin Company, 1964.

Bering, Henrik. *Outpost Berlin: The History of the Allied Military Forces in Berlin 1945–1994.* Chicago: Edition Q, Inc., 1995.

Beschloss, Michael R. *The Crisis Years: Kennedy & Khrushchev 1960–1963.* New York: Edward Burlingame Books, c1991.

Blair, Jean, and Clay Blair. *The Search for JFK.* Berkley: Putnam, 1976.

Bohlen, Charles E. *Witness to History, 1929–1969.* W.W. Norton & Company, Inc., 1973.

Briggs, Asa, ed. *20th-Century World Biography.* Oxford University Press, 1993.

Burns, James MacGregor. *John Kennedy.* Harcourt Brace, 1959.

Carter, Violet Bonham. *Winston Churchill: An Intimate Portrait.* New York: Harcourt, Brace & World, Inc., 1923.

Chernow, Ron. *The House of Morgan.* Atlantic Monthly Press, 1990.

Churchill, Sir Winston. *The World Crisis.* Scribner, 1927.

Davis, John H. *The Kennedys: Dynasty & Disaster.* McGraw Hill, 1987.

Eisenhower, Dwight D. *Crusade in Europe.* Doubleday & Company, Inc., 1948.

Foster, R.F. *Modern Ireland: 1600–1972.* The Penguin Press, 1988.

Fromkin, David. *In the Time of the Americans.* New York: Alfred A. Knopf, 1995.

Gilbert, Martin, ed. *Churchill: Great Lives Observed.* Prentice Hall, 1967.

Gilbert, Martin. *At The Admiralty: September 1939–May 1940.* Vol. 1 of *The Churchill War Papers.* New York and London: W.W. Norton & Company, Inc.

Grove, Eric. *Sea Battles: In Close-Up, World War II.* Vol. 2. Naval Institute Press, 1993.

Hamilton, Nigel. *JFK: Reckless Youth.* Random House, 1992.

Hopper, Bruce. *Pan Sovietism.* Boston: Houghton Mifflin Company, 1931.

Howley, Frank. *Berlin Command.* New York: G.P. Putnam & Sons, 1950.

Kennedy, John F. *The Strategy of Peace.* Harper & Brothers, 1960.

Kennedy, John F. *Why England Slept.* W. Funk, Inc., 1940.

Krock, Arthur. *Memories.* New York: Funk & Wagnalls, 1968.

Manchester, William. *Death of a President.* Harper & Row, 1967.

Manchester, William. *One Brief Shining Moment.* Boston and Toronto: Little, Brown and Company, 1983.

Manchester, William. *Portrait of a President.* Little Brown, 1962.

Manchester, William. *The Last Lion: Winston Spencer Churchill, Alone 1932–1940.* Little, Brown and Company, 1988.

McCullough, David. *Truman.* Simon & Schuster, 1992.

Millis, Walter, ed. *The Forrestal Diaries.* The Viking Press, 1951.

Morison, Samuel Eliot. *The Atlantic Battle Won: May 1943–May 1945.* Vol. 10 of *History of United States Naval Operations in World War II.* Boston: Little, Brown and Company, 1956.

Nunnerly, David. *President Kennedy & Britain.* New York: St. Martin's Press, 1972.

O'Brien, Máire, and Conor Cruise O'Brien. *A Concise History of Ireland.* New York: Beekman House, 1972.

O'Donnell, Kenneth P., and David F. Powers. *Johnny, We Hardly Knew Ye: Memories of John Fitzgerald Kennedy.* Boston: Little, Brown and Company, 1972.

Parmet, Herbert S. *Jack: The Struggles of John F. Kennedy.* New York: The Dial Press.

Parmet, Herbert S. *JFK: The Presidency of John F. Kennedy.* New York: The Dial Press.

Sidey, Hugh. *John F. Kennedy: President.* Atheneum, 1963.

Sidey, Hugh. *The Memories: JFK, 1961–1963.* New York: W.W. Norton & Company, Inc., 1963.

Strober, Gerald S., and Deborah H. Strober. *Let Us Begin Anew: An Oral History of the Kennedy Presidency.* Harper Perenniel, 1993.

Truman, Margaret. *Harry S. Truman.* New York: William Morrow & Company, Inc., 1973.

Weintraub, Stanley. *The Last Great Victory: The End of World War II, July/August 1945.* New York: Dutton, 1995.

Whalen, Richard J. *The Founding Fathers.* Regnery Publishing, Inc., 1964.

Wheeler-Bennett, Sir John, and Anthony Nicholls. *The Semblance of Peace.* New York: St. Martin's Press, 1972.

Ziegler, Philip. *London At War: 1939–1945.* Alfred A. Knopf, 1995.

Ziegler, Philip. *Mountbatten: A Biography.* New York: Alfred A. Knopf, 1985.

INDEX

Jarley

Annarette pan[...]
became — We do[...]
heart cruelu c[...]

") he no greer fa[...]
is the gover [...]

Mr. Bruce